# DATE DUE

| | | | |
|---|---|---|---|
| JE 18 '93 | | | |
| SE 23 '94 | | | |
| DE 23 '94 | | | |
| AP 17 '95 | | | |
| DE 13 '96 | | | |
| NO 1 '97 | | | |
| OV 28 '98 | | | |
| NO 19 '98 | | | |
| AP 17 '04 | | | |
| MY 11 '04 | | | |
| AP 20 '05 | | | |
| | | | |
| NO 7 '05 | | | |
| FE '06 | | | |
| | | | |
| | | | |
| | | | |
| | | | |

# Mexican American Theater:
## Legacy and Reality

## Nicolás Kanellos

### Latin American Literary Review Press

### Pittsburgh

**1987**

# Acknowledgements

With the exception of one, all of the essays included here were first published in various scholarly journals and anthologies: "Chicano Theater in the Seventies," *Theater* (Journal of the Yale School of Drama) 12/1 (Fall-Winter, 1980); "Chicano Theater as Folklore and Folklore in Chicano Theater," *Journal of the Folklore Institute* 15/1 (January-April, 1978); "Chicano Theater: A Popular Culture Battleground," *Journal of Popular Culture* 13/3 (Spring, 1980); "A Brief Overview of the Mexican-American Circus in the Southwest," *Journal of Popular Culture* 18/2 (Fall, 1985); "The Mexican Stage in the Southwestern United States as a Sounding Board for Cultural Conflict," *Missions in Conflict: Essays on U.S.-Mexican Relations and Chicano Culture* (Tübingen, Germany: Gunter Narr Verlag, 1986). "The Origins and Development of Hispanic Theater in the Southwest," is based on two articles: "The Nineteenth Century Origins of the Hispanic Theater in the Southwest," *Crítica* (Spring, 1984) and "The Flourishing of Hispanic Theater in the Southwest," *Latin American Theater Review* 16/1 (Fall, 1983).

This volume is the result of a co-publication agreement of the Spanish-Speaking Outreach Institute of the University of Wisconsin-Milwaukee and Latin American Literary Review Press. My sincerest thanks to Rodolfo Cortina and Yvette Miller for their friendship and support, and to the National Endowment for the Humanities for its support of a portion of the research that is reported in these articles.

Latin American Literary Review Press

P.O. Box 8385

Pittsburgh, PA 15218

Library of Congress Catalog No. 86-15330
ISBN 0-935480-22-6

Printed in the United States of America

This book is dedicated to the indomitable spirit of the players who have persisted in their artistic and activist madness for two centuries. It is also lovingly dedicated to my indomitable wife, Cristelia, who kept pushing me to get this book out.

# Contents

# Chicano Theater in the Seventies

El Teatro Campesino's decade-long pilgrimage through various performance styles appropriately culminated with its writer-director's debut on Broadway. Previous forays into New York and Europe had brought Luis Valdez and El Teatro Campesino recognition as an innovative, agit-prop troupe whose primary concern was the popularizing of the plight of southwestern farmworkers. But by 1968 Valdez and Campesino had left the vineyards and lettuce patches in a conscious effort to create a theater for the Chicano nation, a people envisioned by Valdez and other grass roots organizers of the sixties as working-class, Spanish-speaking or bilingual, rurally oriented and with very strong Pre-Columbian cultural ties. However, Valdez' 1979 Broadway debut departed from this initial orientation in that ZOOT SUIT examined the urban experience of the Chicano and was an attempt at addressing a mass audience on a commercial basis.

By 1970 El Teatro Campesino had pioneered and developed what would come to be known as *teatro chicano*, a style of agit-prop that incorporated the spirit and presentational style of the *commedia dell'arte* with the humor, character types, folklore and popular culture of the Mexican, especially as articulated earlier in the century by Mexican vaudeville companies that toured the Southwest in tent theaters.

Almost overnight, groups appeared throughout the United States to continue down the path opened by Valdez. In streets, parks, churches and schools, Chicanos were spreading a newly found bilingual-bicultural identity through the *actos*, one-act pieces introduced by Valdez that explored all of the issues confronting Mexican Americans: the farmworker struggle for unionization, the Vietnam War, the drive for bilingual education, community control of parks and schools, the war against drug addiction and crime, etc. El Teatro Campesino's *acto, Los Vendidos*, a farcical attack on political manipulation of Chicano stereotypes, could be seen performed by diverse groups from Seattle to Austin. The publication of *Actos by Luis Valdez y el Teatro Campesino*[1] in 1971 placed a ready-made repertoire in the hands of community and student groups and also supplied them with theatrical and political canons:

1. Chicanos must be seen as a nation with geographic, religious, cultural and racial roots in Aztlán. Teatros must further the idea of nationalism and create a national theater based on identification with the Amerindian past.[2]
2. The organizational support of the national theater would be from within, for, "the corazón de la Raza cannot be revolutionized on a grant from Uncle Sam."[3]
3. Most important and valuable of all was that "The teatros must never get away from La Raza . . . . If the Raza will not come to the theater, then the theater must go to the Raza. This, in the long run, will determine the shape, style, content, spirit, and form of el teatro chicano."[4]

El Teatro Campesino's extensive touring, the publicity it gained from the farmworker struggle, and the publication of ACTOS all effectively contributed to the launching of a national *teatro* movement. It reached its peak in the summer of 1976 when five *teatro* festivals were held to counter the gringo bicentennial celebration.[5] The summer's festivals also culminated a period of growth that saw some of Campesino's followers reach sufficient esthetic and political maturity to break away from Valdez. Los Angeles' Teatro Urbano in its mordant satire of American heroes, *Antibicentennial Special*, insisted on intensifying the *teatro* movement's radicalism in the face of Campesino's increasing religious mysticism. Santa Barbara's El Teatro de la Esperanza was achieving perfection, as no other Chicano theater had, in working as a collective and in assimilating the teachings of Brecht in their plays (not *actos*), *Guadalupe* and *La Victima*. San Jose's El Teatro de la Gente had taken the *corrido*-type *acto*, a structure which sets a mimic ballet to traditional Mexican ballads sung by a singer/ narrator, and perfected it as its innovator, El Teatro Campesino, had never done. El Teatro Desengaño del Pueblo from Gary, Indiana, had succeeded in reviving techniques of radical theaters of the

1930's in their *Silent Partners*, an expose of corruption in a local city's construction projects.

The greatest contribution of Luis Valdez and El Teatro Campesino was their inauguration of a true grass roots theater movement. Following Valdez' directions, the university students and community people creating *teatro* held fast to the doctrine of never getting away from the Raza, the grass roots Mexican. In so doing they created the perfect vehicle for communing artistically within their culture and environment. At times they idealized and romanticized the language and the culture of the *mexicano* in the United States. In truth, they discovered a way to mine history, folklore and religion for those elements that could best solidify the heterogeneous community and sensitize it as to class, cultural identity and politics. This indeed was revolutionary. The creation of art from the folk materials of a people, their music, humor, social configurations and environment represented the fulfillment of Luis Valdez' vision of a Chicano national theater.

While Campesino, in its post-UFWOC days, was able to experiment and rediscover the old cultural forms—the *carpas*, the *corridos*, the Guadalupe plays, the *peladito*—it never fully succeeded in combining all of the elements it recovered and invented into a completely refined piece of revolutionary art. LA GRAN CARPA DE LA FAMILIA RASCUACHI was a beautiful creation, incorporating the spirit, history, economy, and music of La Raza. However, its proposal for the resolution of material problems through spiritual means (a superimposed construct of Aztec mythology and Catholicism) seriously marred the work.

It was precisely this contradiction that brought the cultural nationalism of Campesino and the Marxist esthetics of some of the other companies to a head at the Quinto Festival de los Teatros Chicanos held in Mexico City in 1974. From that point onward, under an intense barrage of criticism from Marxist *teatros* and theater critics, El Teatro Campesino began to withdraw from the organized theater movement. Teatro Nacional de Aztlán (TENAZ), the national theater organization, while keeping its nationalistic name, continued in a leftist direction, but without Luis Valdez. Its greatest triumph as a leftist theater organization occurred in 1976. It succeeded in creating a national forum at the grass roots level through its counter-bicentennial festivals in Los Angeles, Denver, San Jose and Seattle. The organization was also well-represented at the Latin American Theater Festival in New York City, hosted by Teatro Cuatro.

While *teatros* in general were becoming more and more radicalized along Marxist lines, El Teatro Campesino became more and more commercially oriented. Danny Valdez began to appear in Hollywood movies and Luis Valdez set his sights on Broadway. At that point in history, both locations were about as far away from La Raza as one could get. However, it is obvious how important it can be for Chicanos to enter and reform both of these centers of commodity art. But while Teatro Campesino progressed in this direction, many other *teatros* criticized the company as compromising its earlier ideals. But the leftist theaters were also removing themselves from the grass roots to some extent. Excesses and infighting within the Chicano left, particularly among the 'street' Marxists, also resulted in *teatros* disbanding or getting too far from their audiences. A few of the more radical theaters went to the extreme of performing only for audiences composed of initiated leftists. From 1976 to the present, there has been a marked decline in the number of active *teatros*. Some have merged and consolidated; many former *teatro* members have set aside their initial radicalism to pursue the legitimate stage, movies, television or academia.

From the beginnings of El Teatro Campesino in 1965 until 1976, there is a discernible period of proliferation and flourishing in Chicano theatres. Following El Teatro Campesino's retreat from Delano, there is a great emphasis placed upon self-support and self-sufficiency in the movement, with Campesino taking the lead in founding a commune and El Centro Cultural Campesino. Luis Valdez initiated the nationalistic philosophy as a basis for the movement, going to the extreme of reviving pre-Columbian dance-drama as a format for *teatro*. TENAZ was created to institutionalize the growing teatro movement. The organization offered direction, technical assistance, training, bookings for touring groups from Latin America, workshops, festivals, publications, and promoted a high level of professionalism for *teatro*. Even as TENAZ rose to its peak of effectiveness in 1976, it was losing members. El Teatro Campesino had assumed the function of national Chicano touring com-

A scene from the Los Angeles production of *Zoot Suit*.

Esperanza's *Brujerías*.

**El Teatro Campesino**

pany, which had originally been one of TENAZ's intended purposes. In the face of this, TENAZ became an informal administrative and communications organ for *teatros*. In the late 70's TENAZ operations became dependent on government funding and on the university affiliation of its members. To a great extent, the days of *teatro* as an arm of revolutionary nationalism were over. The revolutionary aims of the movement had resulted in modest reforms and certain accomodations. Luis Valdez became a member of the California Arts Council. Many other *teatro* and former *teatro* people were integrated into local arts agencies and boards throughout the Southwest. Former *teatristas* were becoming professors of drama, authors and editors of scholarly books and journals on Chicano literature and theater.

Where once Chicano theater was learned in the fields or in the barrios, today it is more likely to be taken as an accredited course at a university. Playwrights and directors, such as Adrián Vargas, Carlos Morton, Rubén Sierra, and others, now hold the degree of Master of Fine Arts. Morton's plays have been produced more by university-related theater groups than by independent *teatros*. The only two anthologies of Chicano plays have been published by university-based presses, one with a Ford Foundation grant and the other with a grant from the National Endowment for the Arts.[7] *Tenaz Talks Teatro* was a newsletter published at the University of California-San Diego by Professor Jorge Huerta, an officer in TENAZ and one of the organizers of a very successful and highly professional TENAZ festival held in San Diego. Where once *teatros* criss-crossed the countryside to perform without charge at rallies and marches to assist in political organizing, they now tour campuses across the nation, performing for Chicano student groups on regular university programs for fees that are often in excess of $1500 a performance.

Perhaps the academy is serving as a sheltered middle ground, a place insulated from the rigors of the marketplace—a la Broadway—and the political and social demands of the streets. Perhaps the academy is a place where Chicano theater may be pursued and developed as an art form until such a time when it will be ready to compete successfully on the Anglo-dominated national scene. Whatever the motivation, the academy has fostered the second

14

stage in the development of *teatro*. In this stage, professional artistry is as important as the socio-political message. In this way, the previously restrictive nationalism can give way to an openness, where other influences and directions outside of the grass roots culture can be encouraged. Let us not forget that Chicano theater advances into the academy were also spearheaded by Luis Valdez at the University of California, Berkeley, in 1970. It was there that he recruited some of Campesino's members while directing a student theater, Hijos del Sol.

As the decade of the 70's closed, Valdez had already gone to Hollywood and Broadway. Is this the new ground for Chicano theater to conquer in the 1980's? It seems likely, especially when one considers the demographics of the Hispanic community in the United States and the consumer market that they represent. The burgeoning Chicano middle class must be reckoned with, especially by those Chicano theater people who have made their way into the university, and who have, whether they admit it or not, become part of the middle class. Can they continue to cultivate a grass roots art form?

[1]*Actos by Luis Valdez y El Teatro Campesino*. San Juan Bautista: Cucaracha Press, 1971.

[2]Luis Valdez, "Notes on Chicano Theater," in *Actos*, p. 3.

[3]*Ibid*.

[4]*Ibid*, p. 4.

[5]See my review of these festivals, "Séptimo Festival de los Teatros Chicanos," *Latin American Theater Review* 10/1 (Fall, 1976).

[6]Roberto Garza, ed., *Contemporary Chicano Theatre*. Notre Dame: Notre Dame University Press, (1976).

[7]Nicolas Kanellos and Jorge Huerta, eds., *Nuevos Pasos: Chicano and Puerto Rican Drama*. (Gary: *Revista Chicano-Riqueña*, 1979).

# Folklore in Chicano Theater
# and Chicano Theater as Folklore

## Historical Background of the Teatro Movement

The eleven years that have passed since Luis Valdez gathered together a group of striking farmworkers in Delano, California, to create a farmworkers' theater in support of the historic grape boycott and strike, have seen the emergence of numerous Chicano theaters in the Southwest and Midwest, and Puerto Rican theaters in the East. The exact number of Chicano and Puerto Rican theater groups is not known, but certainly must exceed one hundred.[1] These groups have developed from and serve such diverse communities as tomato pickers in New Jersey, factory workers in New York, Chicago and Los Angeles, assembly line workers in Detroit, steelworkers in northwest Indiana, cannery workers in San Jose, and farmworkers throughout the Southwest, Midwest and Northwest. Many of the *teatros* are short-lived and are barely aware of the existence of the majority of their counterparts. Some do not hold regular rehearsals and performances, but meet together occasionally when an important community or Chicano movement issue needs to be dramatized. Only a few groups have achieved stability and manage to operate for as long as five or six years.

Most of the *teatros* share similarities in theme and purpose, but their styles and levels of sophistication vary. They range from the unpolished and homespun of groups like Teatro de la Sierra of rural New Mexico, to the agit-prop,[2] Marxist-Leninist esthetic of Los Angeles' Teatro Movimiento Primavera, to the highly artistic, university-related Teatro de la Esperanza of Santa Barbara. Regardless of their level of sophistication, all of these groups incorporate folkloric material, some consciously and others quite naturally and without any artistic, anthropological or ideological criteria for doing so. In fact, the majority of Chicano theaters in the Southwest and Midwest, and to some extent the Puerto Rican theaters in the East, are folk theaters. They are folk theaters because they unselfconsciously reflect the life, mores and customs of the grass roots communities from which they have sprung, performing mainly for those communities. These theaters not only represent the worldview of their *pueblo*, but often carry on traditional forms of acting, singing and performing. Many times they exhibit the vestiges of various types of folk drama practiced historically by Chicanos and Puerto Ricans.[3]

Some theater groups, instead of being responsive to the issues of their local *barrio* or region, serve a more specialized constituency, for example, Latino high school and college students of a given area, or chapters of a specific Latino political organization, like C.A.S.A., Hermandad General de Trabajadores, or the Raza Unida Party. When such is the case, these theater groups direct their energies to dramatizing the specific issues of the organizations to which they belong. They may explain the finer points of ideology or philosophy which their respective organizations represent. The Teatro Luis Jr. Martínez serves Denver's Crusade for Justice in this manner. Los Angeles' Teatro Movimiento Primavera is the propagandistic and cultural arm of C.A.S.A. However, theater groups of this nature owe less to Chicano and Puerto Rican folk tradition and relate more directly to a regional, national or sometimes international political movement.

The first and only Chicano theater to become a professional company is the Teatro Campesino, which also operates a commune and cultural center in San Juan Bautista, California. The Campesino left the exclusive service of the farmworkers' struggle in 1967 to address broader issues and further develop *teatro* as a Chicano cultural and artistic form.[4] Despite its professionalism, its national and international tours, and its winning of Broadway's highest awards, the Teatro Campesino is still nourished by the folk culture which it represents, although its use of the folklore is now very astute, scientific and purposeful. That is, as the Teatro Campesino has become more artistically sophisticated, it has very carefully selected and elaborated Mexican folk motifs to (1) enlighten its audiences as to the basic elements of Chicano culture, (2) please these audiences by providing material that is not only familiar but cherished, and (3) purposefully create a type of theater that is consistent with Mexican-American tradition. For example, the Teatro Campesino has fully explored the Mexican attitude towards death and its symbolic representation in Mexican folklore and popular culture. Consequently, it created the character, Death, who is ever-present and fatefully manipulates the action in such works as *La Gran Carpa de la Familia Rascuachi*. Heavily inspired by folk customs revolving around the *Día de los Muertos*, as well as by the works of the Mexican engraver and illustrator of *corrido* broadsides, José Guadalupe Posada, Campesino has created this dramatic figure, Death. Campesino also attired its musical ensemble, La Banda Calavera (The Skull Band) in death masks and skeleton costumes, and has illustrated its publications and posters with copies of Posada's work. Also, El Teatro Campesino's experiments with the *corrido* as a dramatic form are a result of this artistic elaboration of folklore. In these and other experiments with Mexican and Mexican-American folk arts and culture, Teatro Campesino has influenced the other Latino theaters in the United States as well as in Mexico. In the eleven years of its existence, El Teatro Campesino has risen from the leadership of a limited and rather unknown group of folk theaters to become one of the leaders of experimental theater arts in the Western world. And today one can truly join the name of Campesino's director and mentor, Luis Valdez,[5] with those of Peter Brook, Jerzy Grotowski, Richard Schecter, Enrique Buenaventura and Augusto Boal.

The early Teatro Campesino functioned in two manners: (1) it promoted solidarity among striking farmworkers and attempted to proselytize strike-breakers; (2) it served as a propaganda organism for the grape boycott among non-farmworkers. The majority of its actors at that time were farmworkers who created their material through improvisations based on their personal and group experiences as farmworkers. Their main audience was constituted of farmworkers like themselves. Thus their *actos*, like *La quinta temporada*,[6] demonstrated the seasonal nature of their work and the need for unionization. The desired effects of the grape boycott were projected in their *Las dos caras del patroncito*. From the beginning, Campesino incorporated the singing of traditional songs into their performances and began changing the words to reflect the

El Teatro de la Gente's *El Cuento de la Migra*

El Teatro de la Sierra's *Narangutang*

reality of the strike. "Se Va el Caimán" became their "El Picket Sign,"[7] whose infectious tune and lyrics have been sung by thousands of striking farmworkers and sympathizers. New songs like "Viva Huelga en General" were soon composed to document the progress of the strike and boycott. Later, some songs and *corridos* would become the bases for their dramatic material.[8]

The Teatro Campesino's most important contribution to the fast-spreading *teatro* movement, however, was the *acto*. The *acto*, which is highly indebted to agit-prop theater and to *commedia dell'arte*,[9] was introduced by Luis Valdez to the farmworkers, who subsequently made it their own. The *acto* is basically a short, flexible, dramatic sketch that communicates directly through the language and culture of the Chicanos in order to present a clear and concise social or political message. Humor, often slapstick, is of the essence as the opposition is satirized. According to Luis Valdez, *actos* are supposed to accomplish the following: "Inspire the audience to social action. Illuminate specific points about social problems. Satirize the opposition. Show or hint at solution. Express what people are feeling."[10] The *acto* is usually improvised by the *teatro* collectively and then reworked into final form. It thus arises from the members' common experiences and reflects in an uncontrived fashion their participation in the culture and folklore of their communities.

Because of the *acto*'s flexibility and its introduction as a grass roots Chicano theatrical form, it soon became the dramatic vehicle for the varied experiences of Mexican Americans, not only in the fields of the Southwest, but also in factories and steel mills, on college campuses, and even on the welfare rolls, as shall be seen later in this paper. Also aiding in the fast growth of the *teatro* movement was the Teatro Campesino's leadership in founding in 1971 the Teatro Nacional de Aztlán (TENAZ),[11] the national organization of *teatros* and the publication of its book of *Actos*. But it must be emphasized that much of *teatro* is learned and transmitted orally and visually without the use of scripts or notes. Very few of the community groups ever use scripts, preferring to improvise their material collectively and then memorize the parts. It is an effective means, quite suited to *teatro's* spontaneity and its objective of remaining up-to-date and tailoring performances to specific audiences. But of course this procedure also makes for an ephemeral and easily lost body of dramatic work. It is easy to see that for most of these groups, creating a lasting dramatic statement is far from their minds. Nor are most of the groups mindful of the need to circulate their works so that other *teatros* may adopt them. Much of the material developed by Campesino and other theaters has been imitated or adapted in oral form only. I remember how, as a member of the Teatro Chicano de Austin, I learned my first role in *Los Vendidos* an *acto* "borrowed" from Campesino. We called it the *Tex-Mex Curio Shop*. I learned my role only by copying its enactment by the director, Juan Chavira, without the benefit of a script or notes, or of ever having seen the Teatro Campesino. It was not uncommon in those days—and this is still true for many *teatros*—for one member of our group to teach us an *acto* from memory that he had seen performed by another *teatro*. And this was how other *teatros* adapted some of our own original material. In fact, I was surprised to find material that our group had created in Texas being performed by other *teatros* as far away as Seattle.

Theater members seem to be highly mobile and the theaters themselves suffer from a continuous turn-over in personnel. Thus, the directors have the additional responsibility of teaching new members the roles that have been vacated. Often, members who leave a theater for one reason or another establish new theaters of their own or become members of another theater group. In most cases they bring material from their former group to share with the new one. This was my case when I moved from Texas to Indiana. In my theater baggage I brought three or four *actos* which I taught orally to the Teatro Desengaño del Pueblo in Gary.

The oral nature of *teatro* transmission is also apparent in the way community groups, not *teatros*, adopt an *acto* to perform on their own. For example, the Teatro Chicano de Austin had developed various *actos* to support the national boycott of lettuce for the United Farmworkers Organizing Committee. The local UFWOC workers, after seeing the *actos* performed at a rally, learned the material and began performing the skits on picketlines in front of supermarkets. This also occurs, of course, with the *corridos* that *teatros* compose and sing. In fact, many *teatros* provide sheets of lyrics to assist audiences in singing along.

# A Short Survey of Latino Folk Theaters

While many *teatros* began by performing Teatro Campesino material, the groups that were most closely tied to their own communities soon developed their own material by adapting Campesino's style and the *acto* to their own socio-political reality, a reality that was more often than not an urban one. Such was the case with groups like El Teatro Chicano de Austin, Gary's Teatro Desengaño del Pueblo, Chicago's Teatro Trucha, Denver's Su Teatro and Teatro la Causa de los Pobres, Los Angeles' Teatro Urbano, Tierra Amarilla's Teatro de la Sierra, and Camden's Teatro Alma Latina.

El Teatro Chicano de Austin was founded and directed by Juan Chavira in 1969 after he had worked with a farmworker theater in the Rio Grande Valley of Texas. The group combined University of Texas students and high school students from East Austin. While continuing to perform works relevant to the farmworker struggle and life in South Texas, the group gradually developed material that was more oriented to East Austin. Much of the new material propagandized the need for bilingual education and the teaching of Chicano history and culture in the schools. This was accomplished through the short, satirical schoolroom scenes of *Escuela, High School* and *Brainwash*. Discrimination in local hospital emergency services was attacked in *Hospital*, while *Juan Pistolas* satirized police mistreatment of Chicanos. The group also supported local Mexican American candidates for election to the city council and became heavily involved in voter registration drives. The burlesque of the politician and his campaign practices in one *acto*, and the demonstration of the need for Chicano poll watchers in another became so well known that during election time the group was called to perform not only throughout East Austin, but in neighboring towns and cities whose Chicano citizens were beginning to organize for political representation. Like many other *teatros*, El Teatro Chicano was ready to improvise *actos* on issues that emerged overnight, such as the police killing of an unarmed teenager in East Austin, racist incidents at a local Catholic church, a local furniture workers' strike, a rally against the practices of the federal government's Housing and Urban Development Program (in San Antonio), and various protest marches. While the group's main sphere of activity was Austin, it was often called to perform in neighboring towns and as far away as San Antonio, Dallas and Houston. Once the group made the long trip to perform in Eagle Pass and on another occasion traveled to Washington, D.C., where it had been invited to perform at the American Folklife Festival held by the Smithsonian Institute. Today the members that were formerly high school students have inherited the group and converted it into a theater that serves mainly the needs of Chicano students at the University of Texas at Austin.

El Teatro Desengaño del Pueblo was founded in Gary in 1972 by this author and a combination of Indiana University Northwest students and non-students from the surrounding community. Over the past four years, Desengaño has lost most of its student membership and is presently made up of community people ranging in age from five to forty. But even when the group was dominated by students, they were non-traditional students who were often full-time steelworkers, besides being registered students at the urban, non-residential campus. From the outset, the group created material not on student life but on life in Gary and East Chicago as seen by the Mexican, Chicano and Puerto Rican residents. Desengaño dramatized community issues like Chicano and Puerto Rican unity in *Frijol y Habichuela*, discrimination in employment in *The Employment Office*, the need for bilingual-bicultural education in *Escuela* and *Brainwash*, drugs in *Juan Bobo*, local politics in *La Politica* and *El Alcalde*, dehumanizing work in the steel mills in *Burundanga*. Other material was designed to provide a sense of history, culture, and identity through *teatro: Papá México, El Grito de Lares, Identity* and *Baile*. Like El Teatro Chicano de Austin, Desengaño performs extensively throughout the community at rallies, holiday celebrations, schools, churches and parks. But the group has also traveled throughout the Midwest, performing for the little Mexican colonies in Ohio and Wisconsin, and at universities in Indiana, Illinois, Wisconsin and Michigan. A long, protracted struggle in which the group has been invovled is the battle for the establishment of bilingual-bicultural education in northwest Indiana. Over the past four years the group has performed for teachers,

P.T.A.'s, conferences and rallies in an effort to sensitize the populace and the public institutions to the educational needs of Latinos. Desengaño has also been a faithful member of TENAZ and attended festivals as far away as Mexico City, Los Angeles, San Antonio and Seattle.[12]

Founded in 1973, Compañía Trucha of Chicago's Eighteenth Street *barrio*, began as a very earthy and raucous satirical group that was associated with the Casa Aztlán Community Center. Hard-hitting but humorous satire, through a style that is as unsophisticated as it is relevant and direct to the people of the *barrio*, is Trucha's stock in trade. The ills of urban life, monotonous and dangerous factory work, and dramatizations of actual events fill their *actos*. In one of their pieces a local Mexican entrepeneur's exploitation of illegal Mexican labor, and of community radio and television, is satirized in such a direct and outrageously funny manner that the *barrio* audience's instant recognition and delight fulfills the highest expectations of direct concrete relevance of this type of theater. In another *acto, El Léon y los Crickets*, the people's struggle as a minority within the United States is allegorized through a timeless folktale. Their current *acto, El Hospital de San Lucas*, is the result of their work with a community organization that is making demands on St. Luke's Presbyterian Hospital to serve the needs of the *barrio* in which it is located. Compañía Trucha is one of the local theaters that has weathered the storm of leftist organizations and protest theaters that have tried to transform such grass roots theaters into more sophisticated "cultural arms" of the international class struggle. While at one point swayed to produce more ideological drama, Trucha has returned to its original role in the community and its authentic style.

Two theaters in Denver, Su Teatro and Teatro la Causa de los Pobres, work extensively within their own communities. Su Teatro, while originating as a student group that applied Aztec and Mayan mythology to contemporary issues, has gradually redirected its efforts towards the dramatization of community issues. Its latest work, *El corrido de Auraria*, relives the tragedy of the destruction of some of its own members' former neighborhood, Auraria, to make way for the building of a college. Ironically, one street of the *barrio* was preserved in the middle of the new campus to serve as

**El Teatro la Causa de los Pobres**

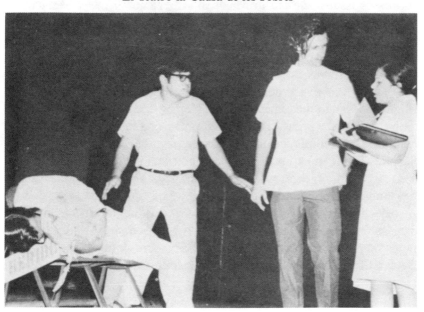

**El Teatro Chicano de Austin in *El Hospital***

faculty offices and as a "living monument to historic Denver." La Causa de los Pobres, on the other hand, is made up of welfare mothers and their children. It began as an expression of Denver's Chicano Welfare Rights Organization and continues to dramatize the injustices of the welfare system that the poor mothers—there are no men in the group—continue to experience in their daily lives. The group's natural concern of course is with its children and their development. La Causa de los Pobres' material, therefore, criticizes not only the welfare system but the schools and the police as well. Drawn from life are their outlandish and biting parodies of such people as the superintendent of schools, Chief of Police Dill (Sour Pickle), and school board member, Mrs. Bradford (Mrs. Bratfart).

More rurally oriented than the others are New Mexico's Teatro de la Sierra and South Jersey's Teatro Alma Latina. Sierra is made up mostly of high school students along with a few other people ranging in age from five to thirty. Once again in a *rascuachi*[13] (down to earth and unsophisticated) but direct manner, this group addresses issues relevant to Mexican Americans in New Mexico's Tierra Amarilla region. Its current *acto, Narangutang*, is an exposure of a corrupt, *caudillo*-type sheriff, and of the lack of community services, like paved streets. El Teatro Alma Latina, on the other hand, serves Puerto Rican agrigultural workers in South Jersey. Their *El emigrao* demonstrates why Puerto Ricans leave their island to work in the tomato fields of Jersey and shows their exploitation by agri-business. Their other *actos* dramatize poor working conditions, unemployment, and abuses by the State Employment Service. Their most imaginative and comical satire is expressed in their exposure of the *espiritistas* (spiritualists or mediums) that take advantage of the Puerto Rican laborers, especially around payday.

Each of these groups, as well as the more experienced and professionalized theaters, has in one way or another used various types of folklore in communicating their socio-political messages. By far the most popular and effective folkloric media adapted by *teatros* are the *corrido* and the *cuento*. In addition, *teatros* emulate popular language patterns, diction and dialects, and enrich their theatrical language with popular phrases, sayings and proverbs. *Teatros* also make use of folkloric artifacts like masks, costumes and musical instruments.

26

# The Corrido

From the beginning, Chicano theaters have combined singing with their dramatic presentations to warm up the audience in preparation for the *actos*, to create variety, or to reinforce the themes presented in the *actos* themselves. The usual reason given for the incorporation of *corridos* was that the *barrio* audience liked them and, if copies of the songs were handed out to the audience, people would sing along. The *corridos*, especially the border ballads and the ones that deal with historical themes, also coincided in spirit and impact with a great deal of *teatro* material. A few *teatros*, moreover, were fortunate enough to have as members *corridistas* or composers of *corridos*. They in turn had in *teatro* a great means of distributing their compositions which at times gained for them a minor following and the opportunity to have their songs recorded. The most famous of the *teatro* composers are Agustin Lira and Daniel Valdez[14] of Teatro Campesino, Ramon Moroyoqui Sánchez (Chunky),[15] formerly of Teatro Mestizo, and Rumel Fuentes,[16] formerly of Teatro Chicano de Austin.

The *corrido* in Chicano theater became so important that in 1971 TENAZ sponsored a workshop on the *corrido* and the ways of incorporating it into *teatro* performances. In truth, many *teatros* had already been experimenting with the incorporation of the *corrido* into the *actos* themselves. Some, like Seattle's Teatro del Piojo, had presented tableaus of the Mexican Revolution through the dramatization and singing of the most famous *corridos* from the Revolution. Others, like the *teatro* of the Colegio Jacinto Treviño in Texas, created abstract mimic routines to *corridos* like "Valentín de la Sierra." The Teatro Chicano de Austin indicted the power of Texas ranchers and their use of the Texas Rangers to subdue Mexican Americans who once owned the ranchers' lands. The *teatro* turned the tables on the ranchers and the rangers by bringing to life the hero of the "Corrido de Jacinto Treviño," who was treated as an historical personage. The *acto* would begin with the singing of the "Corrido de Jacinto Treviño," followed by a monologue in which a rancher gloated over his lands, power and wealth. The rancher

27

would then train two dumb, doglike Texas Rangers to attack Chicanos and Blacks. When the rangers attacked picketing farmworkers, from backstage would be heard the following verse of the *corrido*:

> Entrenle, rinches cobardes.
> El pleito no es con un niño,
> Quieren conocer su padre.
> Yo soy Jacinto Treviño.

> Come on in, you cowardly rangers.
> You're not dealing with a child.
> Come and meet your father.
> I am Jacinto Treviño.

As this verse is sung, Jacinto Treviño himself comes on stage with guns-a-blazing and, after being confronted by the rangers who grab him by the lapels (as in the *corrido*), he shoots them dead. The *corrido* is once again sung, this time with the audience joining in.

It was the Teatro Campesino, however, that pioneered the *corrido* as a dramatic form and demonstrated its artistic and cultural possibilities in one of its finest works, *La Gran Carpa de la Familia Rascuachi*.[17] The *Gran Carpa* is a very fast paced collage of scenes that follow three generations of an archetypal Chicano family. A series of *corridos* provide the narration to the action and create the rhythm and mood to which the actors execute their mime and dance. The *Gran Carpa* has been performed throughout the nation and abroad, and has been strongly influential in popularizing the *corrido* dramatic technique. Another work by El Teatro Campesino, *El Corrido*, has also had great impact, mainly due to its nation-wide television broadcast.

The *Gran Carpa* is not, however, the best example of the *corrido* as a dramatic form; it is too extensive and disperse. El Teatro de la Gente's *Corrido de Juan Endrogado*, written by director Adrián Vargas, is the finest illustration of the *corrido*'s formalistic qualities. It is a light, dramatic piece whose performance consists of constant mime and dance movement to the beat of the *corridos* and other songs which provide the narration. The actors wear exaggerated makeup, as the *corrido* is designed to depart from realism; for the *corrido* is lyrical, satirical, lightly philosophical and somewhat reminiscent of ballet. As the *corrido* concentrates on themes already familiar to the *barrio*, it can help to coalesce the public's opinion on the matters at hand, but it is in no way comparable to the directness of the agitprop *acto*. The *corrido* wins over the audience with the use of familiar songs, esthetically attractive costumes and acting style, and the creation of easily recognizable scenes and situations. As in the *acto*, there is no scenery and props are minimal.

*El Corrido de Juan Endrogado* accomplishes these objectives delightfully and still manages to deal with the important theme of Mexican-American addiction to the ever-elusive American Dream. *Juan Endrogado* takes as its musical theme the well-known and very popular "Corrido de Juan Charrasqueado," a ballad which recounts the life and death of a hard-drinking, hard-loving gambler. Vargas changed the lyrics to tell the story of Juan Endrogado (John Drugged), a poor man who becomes addicted to the pursuit of the American Dream, with its enticing material symbols and sexual fantasies: high-paying jobs, beautiful cars, fast women. . . . Juan, after failing to attain these, achieves his dreams only in the stupor of drugs. But along with the addict's highs come the waking nightmares of withdrawal, theft to finance the habit, hunger and ultimately, death.

Throughout the piece, which is interspersed with only sparse dialogue, the thematic music returns with the narrative line. *Juan Endrogado* opens with the singing of these lines which can be compared to the original "Corrido de Juan Charrasqueado":

*Juan Endrogado*
Voy a cantarles un corrido de mi pueblo,
lo que ha pasado muchas veces por acá,
la triste historia de un hermano endrogado
que por poquito con las drogas se mataba.

I'm going to sing you a *corrido* of my people,
about something that happens often out here,
the story of a dope-addicted brother,
who little by little was killing himself with drugs.

*Juan Charrasqueado*
Voy a cantarles un corrido muy mentado,
lo que ha pasado en la hacienda de la Flor,
la triste historia de un ranchero enamorado
que fue borracho, parrandero y jugador.

I'm going to sing a *corrido* that's quite famous,
about what happened at the Hacienda de la Flor,
the sad tale of an enamoured rancher
who was a drinker, a good-time Charlie and a gambler.

As the play progresses, the new *corrido* becomes less and less
like its model, and other types of songs are introduced to corres-
pond in theme and mood with the action. At times the music is
very somber and elegiac; other times it is fast and happy and the
actors must keep pace by almost doing a two-step or a polka. Included in the repertoire of songs used and transformed in the play
are these very popular numbers: "Cuanto Sufro en esta Vida" (ran-
chera), "El Muchacho Alegre" (corrido), "Creí" (bolero), "Put
on Your Red Dress" (rock and roll) and the melody to a Chevrolet
television and radio commercial.

All of the lyrics, tunes and actions are perfectly synchronized.
At times, a song's original lyrics are not transformed *per se* but are
used to create stage irony. This is so with "A Medias de la Noche."
It is sung to a scene where Juan is seized with hunger pains and the
song's original lyrics take on a new, ironic meaning. It is no longer
a loved one that is embracing Juan, as in the song, but Hunger
herself:

A medias de la noche te soñaba.
Te soñaba abrazándote conmigo.
Te soñaba abrazándote conmigo,
pero ay qué angustia
me ha dejado esta mujer!

Around midnight I was dreaming of you.
I dreamed that you were embracing me.
I dreamed that you were embracing me,
but oh what anguish

this woman has caused me!

Thus, the *corrido* is a dramatic piece that brings the audience and actors close together. The *barrio* audiences have lived with these songs and love them. Both the actors and the audience, through the performance, are joined in a type of poetic union that arises spontaneously from the shared values and experiences. The *corrido* as a dramatic form is an innovation in Chicano theater, but hardly a departure from tradition.

As yet, the Puerto Rican popular theaters have not drawn this type of format from Puerto Rican folk or popular music. However, the theaters are at a point where *plenas* are incorporated into the *actos* to illustrate the main themes. Teatro Alma Latina of Camden, in its *El Emigrao*, includes a *plena* as background narration for the play's action. This is the first of four stanzas that they have composed:

Esta es la historia, señores,
de un jíbaro borincano
que salió pa los nuyores
con un bolsito en la mano.

This is the story, people,
of a Puerto Rican hillbilly
who departed for New York
with but a little sack in his hands.

The Teatro Guazabara that works out of Livingston College in New Jersey also incorporates *plenas* into such works as *Los Obreros Migrantes*. The following *plena*-like song serves as narrative background and lends an epic dimension to the scene which depicts the exodus of migrant workers at the San Juan airport:

Ya se van, ya se van, ya se van.
Los boricuas engañados ya se van.
(Stanza is repeated.)

Por las necesidades
que reinan en sus hogares
se emigran a los tomatales

donde reina la injusticia
del Farmer dictatorial.

Ya se van, etc.

There they go, there they go, there they go.
There go those deceived Puerto Ricans.

Because of the poverty that reigns in their homes
they emigrate to the tomato fields
where reigns the injustice
of the dictatorial Farmer.


## Folktales, Legends, and Personal Experience Narratives


*Teatros* throughout the country use several types of folk narrative techniques and structures in their works because their audiences are familiar with traditional types of oral communication. In Mexican folk culture, the *cuento* or tale has often been used to illustrate a moral or practical lesson. It is quite natural that Chicano theaters appropriate the *cuento* as a means of furthering the didactic purposes of the *acto*.

At a rally in Austin, César Chávez illustrated the need for unity among Chicanos by telling the tale of "Las Avispas." The Teatro Chicano de Austin, immediately impressed by the lesson and the form that it took, soon thereafter transformed the tale into a dramatic piece.[18] This tale, which deals with the skill of an expert whip handler who tyrannizes all the animals of the forest, except the wasps (does not mean White Anglo-Saxon Protestant), who are organized, was also adopted by Mexico's Teatro Mascarones quite independently of César Chávez and Chicano theater. Los Mascarones used the tale to demonstrate the need for unity and organization to *campesinos* in Southern Mexico. Under similar circumstances, the Compañia Trucha heard Reies Tijerina use the tale of "El León y los Crickets." As mentioned above, Trucha gave the lion the identity of the dominant society in the United States, and the poor, powerless, little crickets became the Chicanos.

Many of the *teatros* have dramatized legends or helped to further elaborate them. The best known and most dramatized legend is that of La Llorona, the Crying Lady. Legendary figures like Emiliano Zapata, Pancho Villa and now Che Guevara continue to appear or be invoked in *actos* from coast to coast. Beyond the legend, religious figures taken directly from the miracle plays and *pastorelas* have also made their way into *teatro*. San Antonio's Teatro de Artes Chicanos used to perform an allegory of a Poor Man, God, Death and the Devil (complete with the devil's mask and costume from the *pastorela*). The Teatro Campesino and a few other groups annually produce the Virgin of Guadalupe miracle play for their local parishes on the Mexican patron saint's feast day.

*Teatros* have not only recreated and adapted certain folktales and legends, but also have appropriated various folk figures like Pantaleón, Juan Pistolas, el Pelado and Juan Bobo and placed them in new, urban surroundings. The *teatros* have also helped to solidify the characters of various other popular stereotypes like the Pachuco, the Vendido, the Coyote and the Militante that have appeared in contemporary times. El Teatro Chicano de Austin characterized Pantaleón Manso as an unsuspecting, gullible Chicano who falls prey to the scheme of the ghetto used car, electrical appliance and real estate salesmen. El Teatro Campesino based its *Carpa Cantinflesca* and its *La Gran Carpa de la Familia Rascuachi* on the poverty-stricken, luckless character known in Mexico as *el pelado* ("the naked one") and made famous by the world-renowned comedian, Cantinflas. The Teatro Desengaño made use of Puerto Rico's most famous picaresque figure, Juan Bobo, in an *acto* designed to show teenagers that taking drugs is dumb.

Certain popular stereotypes have been forming in the course of the development of Chicano culture in the United States and they have steadily made their way into Chicano theater scenes. First and foremost of these popular figures is the Pachuco or zoot-suiter, the teenage rebel who developed his own subculture in the forties and fifties. Almost every *teatro* has at one time or another paraded this swaggering, marijuana-smoking, *caló*-speaking[19] hipster on its stage. Another character that was ubiquitous in early Chicano theater was the Vendido or Sell-Out, sometimes referred to as Tío Taco. He was the Mexican American that was bought by the System to deal with his own kind or serve as token minority representation. The Coyote, of long tradition in the *corridos* that deal with Mexican labor in the United States, is the despicable labor contractor who exploits his own brothers on both sides of the border with his illegal gambit. The Militante is of course a parody of young Chicano militants who are seen as being very loud and menacing but assimilated to the dominant culture and thus rendered ineffective. Many of these character types are represented in El Teatro Campesino's *Los Vendidos*, as robots for sale to the governor of California, who is in need of someone to get him the Mexican American vote. Also included in this *acto* is the Frito Bandito, Frito-Lay's corn chip bandit that has served as a gross stereotype of Mexicans in the mass media.

Chicano and Puerto Rican theaters have also taken the personal experience narrative as a basis for some of their work. New York's Teatro Calle 4 conducted a series of interviews with Puerto Ricans on the Lower East Side in preparing their *Que Encontraste en Nueva york?* The result is a work that follows the misfortunes of a newly arrived *jíbaro*, a country-bumpkin who gets a rude awakening as an introduction to life in the New York ghettoes. He is duped, robbed, beaten and finally becomes disillusioned. He resembles the protagonists of many a joke or tale about the transition from the Caribbean "paradise" to the urban jungle.

El Teatro de la Gente's *El Cuento de la Migra* is the story of an illegal immigrant from Mexico and his misfortunes at the hands of the border patrol, the labor contractor, the factory owner and the Immigration and Naturalization Service. The *acto* begins with the following *corrido* stanza as historical background:

Año de mil ochocientos
cuarenta y ocho corría
firmaron dos gobernantes
y a mi pueblo dividían.

In the year eighteen hundred
and forty-eight
two rulers signed a contract
and divided my people.

This is followed by a monologue which affects the style and speech patterns of an old-timer relating his personal experiences:

y desde ese entonces ha existido esa frontera por allí por el sur. Sí, pero una frontera muy caprichosa, no reconocida por el pueblo mexicano trabajador. Y si a mí me dicen que soy espalda mojada porque crucé un río asina de ancho, bien se sabrá el super-espalda mojada quien cruzó ese marezote. Sí, señor, porque a estas tierras yo he venido. También de estas tierras yo he nacido. Por eso les vengo a contar este cuento, el cuento de la migra. Sí, señor, esa víbora, ese animal que en estos días les está dando en la madre a nuestra madre. El cuento comienza en mil novecientos setenta cuando de repente, ¡Ahi viene la migra![20]

This example of the personal experience style, as well as the other examples of narrative techniques used by *teatros*, illustrates popular theater's attempts to communicate in the vernacular and to employ performance techniques that are familiar to Latino communities throughout the United States.

## Language and Language Usage

The context in which a *teatro* uses English or Spanish is an extremely complex matter and depends on many variables, including the Spanish-English language dominance of the community and the dialects in use, the Spanish-English language dominance of the theater members, the social context of the *acto*, and the type of character that is speaking. Generally speaking, *teatros* use the language of their audiences, unless typing a character through dialect and other speech patterns. Various degrees of dominance of Spanish and English are represented in the communities and can depend on such factors as the length of time the individual community members have resided in the United States, their age and amount of schooling, or simply their language preference. The Puerto Rican *teatros* in New York and New Jersey use Spanish almost exclusively. Most of the Chicano theaters perform bilingually and have devised various strategies to deal with community language diversity. As always, *teatro* performances are flexible and subject to improvisation on the spot. Thus accommodations in language as well as content are often made during performances.

However complex the problem of bilingualism may be, *teatros* exhibit a gusto for oral expression that manifests itself not only in a richness of popular sayings, phrases and proverbs, but also in experimentation with different dialects and bilingual word play. The heterogeneous make-up of Latino communities is often reflected in *teatro* dialogues. The *caló* of Chicano youth and particularly of the Pachuco, the sing-song accent of immigrants from rural Mexico, the English-Spanish switching of many Southwesterners in particular, the lisping of the Spaniards, the rapid-fire dialect of the Puerto Ricans, the hip language of the New York Ricans, all can be found in the *actos*. El Teatro Desengaño del Pueblo depicts in linguistic form the conflict that has existed between Mexicans and Puerto Ricans in northwest Indiana in their *Frijol y Habichuela*. What is a bean to a Mexican (*frijol*) is not a bean to a Puerto Rican (*habichuela*). The *acto* goes from this initial lexical difference to differences in accent, culture, and race, as the two characters, both of whom are identical beans, fight over their authenticity. After calling each other a series of names which have double meanings within the context of the *acto*, the beans unite and decide that their differences are not great enough to divide them.

*Teatros* explore all of the possibilities that bilingualism offers for creating humor, irony and dramatic conflict. A standard bilingual ploy is the translating of the characters' names from Spanish to English. Such names as Juan Paniaguas, María Dolores de la Barriga and Casimiro Flores are names that approach the ordinary in Spanish. But in English they become John Bread and Water, Mary

Stomach Pains and I Almost See Flowers. An unsympathetic character or a sell-out may be named Ben Dejo (*pendejo* means stupid or naive) or Ben Dido (*vendido* or sell-out). As far as dialogue is concerned, one can imagine the many misunderstandings between Anglos and Latinos that are depicted on stage because of misunderstanding each other's language.

## Professionalism and Sophistication

Since the founding of the national Chicano theater organization (TENAZ) in 1971, a continuous effort has been made towards professionalizing *teatros*. The primary focus of the organization and its leadership, a coordinating council of regional representatives, has been on assisting theaters in developing acting and staging techniques and in creating more esthetically and politically sophisticated material. TENAZ has reached at one time or another probably as many as one hundred theater groups through its annual festivals, regional festivals and workshops. In the course of its existence it has exposed many groups of novices at least to introductory training in body movement, diction, voice, staging, music, puppeteering and mask-making. It has also sponsored seminars, forums and lectures on such diverse topics as Mayan philosophy, Marxist esthetics, cultural nationalism, illegal Mexican immigration, New Mexican land grants, political repression in Latin America and many others. TENAZ has at times also undertaken such projects as video-taping *teatros*, arranging performances for touring Latin American theater companies and publishing a Chicano theater magazine.

A good many *teatros* have taken advantage of some of the TENAZ offerings and have even passed on some of the training to other *teatros* with which they are in contact. Nevertheless, there is also a large number of groups that have looked upon these efforts at professionalization suspiciously and have considered them to be too fancy, too removed from their everyday reality and their issue-oriented theaters. The members of these groups have formed *teatros* not because they consider themselves actors, performers, or artists but because *teatro* is a means of serving their communities in their struggle for civil rights and human dignity. Of the *teatros* studied above, El Teatro Campesino, El Teatro de la Gente, Su Teatro and El Teatro Desengaño have been heavily involved in the TENAZ effort. Groups like the old El Teatro Chicano de Austin, El Teatro Alma Latina, El Teatro de la Sierra, El Teatro de Artes Chicanos de San Antonio and El Teatro de la Causa de los Pobres have remained outside of the influence of TENAZ up until recently. This past summer the Colorado and New Mexican groups attended their first TENAZ festival, which was held in Denver.[21] There they received their first exposure to more sophisticated theaters like El Teatro de la Gente, El Teatro Urbano, and El Teatro de los Niños, from Pasadena, and to workshops on theater techniques and acting. TENAZ, on the other hand, sees only a naive lack of discipline, commitment and organization in those groups that fail to perform up to the level of their artistic potential. While there has always been an apparent respect in *teatros* for the *rascuachi*, TENAZ has had to impose standards of discipline that somewhat remove the organization from the groups that are probably closest to being folk theaters. El Teatro de Artes Chicanos de San Antonio, for example, was turned away from the TENAZ festival in Mexico City in 1965 because it had failed to register in advance. This has occurred quite often because many groups, through their lack of business planning or organization and because they are not professionals, do not spend time corresponding by mail, filling out questionnaires, establishing checking accounts, or even maintaining a permanent address. In many cases, their own performances are arranged strictly by word of mouth. If they decide to attend a festival festival or workshop, they often do so at the last minute possible and often with the idea that they are going basically to perform and to see what the other *teatros* are up to. In many many cases, improving their art or having a study session on radical ical politics is the furthest thing from their minds.

In spite of all these efforts at professionalization, the only *teatro* that has succeeded in becoming a full-time, professional theater is the Teatro Campesino. El Teatro de la Esperanza, a theater group that was the outgrowth of a university program, and El Teatro Movimiento Primavera, the cultural arm of a Marxist organization, are two other groups that have highly developed their theatrical work. For Campesino, professionalism was a goal fostered and realized through the efforts of the university-trained playwright and director, Luis Valdez. It represented the only avenue to a full exploration of the esthetic and cultural possibilities of the Mexican-American theatrical form that Campesino had helped to invent. For Esperanza and Primavera, professionalization has involved a different process.

El Teatro de la Esperanza is one of the most widely known and respected Chicano theaters.[22] In its inception and growth it benefited from support from the Department of Drama at the University of California-Santa Barbara in the form of classes, workshops and a director who was a graduate assistant in drama working on his Ph.D. From the outset, Esperanza was exposed to the most avant-garde dramatic theories and professional training. With these advantages and guidance, Esperanza has been able to take the basic Chicano theatrical form and fully explore its esthetic and political possibilities. Esperanza has become a leader and innovator in Chicano theater not because it has left behind the genuine, the folkloric, the intimate contact with the *pueblo*, but rather because the theater group has taken these elements and perfected them. *Guadalupe*, a documentary one-act play created by the group as a whole, is worthy of consideration as an important contribution to American drama. Today its former director, Jorge Huerta, is a professor of drama at the University of California-San Diego, and Esperanza is faced with the dilemma of continuing to function as an avocational theater for its thoroughly developed actors or as a full-fledged professional theater. There is a definite need for professional Latino theaters and hopefully Esperanza will take the step towards becoming one in the near future.

For Teatro Movimiento Primavera professionalization means attempting to reach the level of artistic control and political ideology exemplified in the works and writings of such models as Bertholt Brecht, Erwin Piscator and Augusto Boal. The group's director, Guillermo Loo, rather than acknowledge the indigenous and folk roots of Chicano theater, emphasizes the influence of the international theater of protest: "We feel that our origins are in the history of scientific proletarian theater."[23] While it is assumed that the ultimate goal of such groups as Primavera is to serve as the cultural and propagandistic arm of a proletarian revolution, their theaters relate more directly to advanced political study groups than to the working classes in the *barrios*. In that they do not have this intimate relationship with the *barrio* and its culture, they find themselves often performing for audiences that are made up of people like themselves: politically sophisticated students or graduates involved in radical political movements of the Left. Their purpose is therefore defeated, as they fail to reach the real working class that is supposed to effect their desired revolution. Groups like Primavera have merely become more specialized in the type of community that they serve. Where once they related to the entire *barrio*, they now serve one segment of the *barrio*, a segment that is probably in transition and in the process of leaving the *barrio*, the young Chicano leftists.

As Chicano and Puerto Rican theaters become more known and accepted, the demand for their performances and their presence within the academic community increases. Because of the solid, popular base that *teatros* have created over the last eleven years, today more and more Chicano and Puerto Rican playwrights are appearing on the contemporary scene, more Chicano and Puerto Rican drama classes are being taught at universities and high schools, and more plays by Latinos are being produced in legitimate theater houses on Broadway, off-Broadway and at universities. The appearance of the playwright in *teatro* is an indication of professionalization in many cases. There is a conversion from collective creation to the specialization of services that is taking place in the most professionalized groups. Luis Valdez was a playwright even before founding the Teatro Campesino, but Campesino did not produce any of his plays before taking that great step to leave the service of the farmworkers' union. Adrián Vargas, after his initial involvement in *teatro*, returned to the university to receive advanced training in playwriting. Groups officially supported by universities, such as El Teatro de la Esperanza, El Teatro Aztlán of California State College at Northridge, the Bilingual Repertory Theater Company at Texas A&I University and Teatro Libre of

Indiana University at Bloomington, have customarily produced plays written by a single member of their group, a well-known Chicano author or a professor at their school. Finally, the playwright without the theater group is also becoming a reality, as a more middle class and academic audience for Latino theater develops. Of course, the works of these writers, which are destined to be performed for a heterogeneous, theater-going public, and by professional actors unknown to the author, have less and less folkloric content. Perhaps as the Latino middle class grows, the need for the type of grass roots theater that has been examined here will diminish and instead Latino life will increasingly be reflected in the mass media, on Broadway and on television. But for now, *teatro* is alive and well in the United States.

[1]For a partial list of Chicano theaters and their addresses, see "TENAZ Directory," *Chicano Theater Three* (1974): 50-54.

[2]According to R. G. Davis, *The San Francisco Mime Troupe: The First Ten Years* (Palo Alto: Rampart Press, 1975), p. 166, agitprop "is agitational propaganda. Agitprop theater is made up of skits performed by people who, like their audience, are directly engaged in the content of the skit. For example: Teatro Campesino, when performing in Delano, California, in 1965-1967, presented agitational propaganda for the members of the Farm Workers Association (NFWA). Their songs and *actos* . . . were designed to inform the workers of union negotiations, grievances and programs. The performers were engaged in organizing work, and their *actos* were extensions of that work."

[3]See my article, "Elementos hispánicos en el teatro chicano," *Actas del XVII Congreso del Instituto Internacional de Literatura Iberoamericana* (Madrid: Centro Iberoamericano de Cooperación, 1978).

[4]For a detailed history of the Teatro Campesino, see Francoise Kourilsky, "Approaching Quetzalcoatl. The Evolution of El Teatro Campesino," *Performance 7* (1973): 37-46.

[5]Sylvia Drake compares Luis Valdez to Jean-Louis Barrault and Francois Rabelais in: "El Teatro Campesino: Keeping the Revolution on Stage," *Performing Arts 8* (September, 1970): p.56. R. G. Davis, in *The San Francisco Mime Troupe*, compares at length the work of Luis Valdez with that of *the* five other radical

41

theater directors: Joe Chaiken, Richard Schecter, Julian Beck, Peter Schumann and himself.

[6]*La Quinta Temporada*, as well as *Las Dos Caras del Patroncito, Los Vendidos* and *Huelguistas*, mentioned below, were published in: *Actos by Luis Valdez y el Teatro Campesino* (Fresno: Cucaracha Press, 1971).

[7]Most people are unaware that the lyrics to "El Picket Sign" and "Viva Huelga en General" were composed by Luis Valdez. They are included in a Teatro Campesino songbook published in mimeograph, circa 1967-71: *Cancionero de la Raza* (Fresno: Teatro Campesino, s.d.). They have also circulated anonymously in hundreds of songsheets and songbooks distributed free or sold by *teatros* throughout the country.

[8]See Luis Valdez, "Huelguistas," ACTOS, pp.99-103.

[9]Prior to founding El Teatro Campesino, Luis Valdez worked with the San Francisco Mime Troupe, where he learned some of the agitprop techniques that he would later apply in *teatro*. He also performed in the Troupe's *commedia* style performance of Lope de Rueda's sixteenth century *paso* (the Spanish version of the *commedia*), *Las Aceitunas*. See Jorge Huerta, "Concerning Teatro Chicano," *Latin American Theater Review 6* (Spring, 1973): p. 15.

[10]Luis Valdez, "The Actos," *Actos*, p. 6.

[11]TENAZ was founded at the first conference of Chicano theater directors held in Fresno, California in 1971 and sponsored by El Teatro Campesino.

[12]During the last two years El Teatro Desengaño del Pueblo has become increasingly more professionalized and sophisticated. Its current production, in fact, is a play, *Silent Partners*, written entirely by its director rather than by the group as a whole.

[13]The term *rascuache* is defined by Francisco J. Santamaría, *Diccionario de mejicanismos* (Mexico City: Editorial Porrúa, 1974), as an adjective meaning "Miserable, ruin, pobre;" that, is, it is usually a miserable, run-down or poor place. The term used by *teatros*, however, is often applied to the poor people of the *barrios*, or their poor, earthy or unsophisticated lifestyle. Many *teatros* have preferred to spell the word *rasquachi*, either in deference to its Aztec derivation or because of the influence of English orthography. Its termination in *i*, instead of *e*, in my text and in *teatro* usage is related to the word's common pronunciation.

[14]Songs by Agustín Lira and Daniel Valdez are included in the *Cancionero de la Raza* cited in note 7. An album of Valdez's songs, "Mestizo," (CAM Records Sp-3622) was recorded in 1974 and is sold at *teatro* performances.

[15]A few *corridos* by Chunky were published anonymously in Teatro Mestizo's songbook, *Cantos Rebeldes de América* (San Diego: Toletcas en Aztlán, 1974). The lyrics to his "La Guitarra Campesina" and "El Corrido Rasquachi" were published in *Revista Chicano-Riqueña* Vol. 2 (Summer, 1974): 4-5.

[16]The words and music to a few of Rumel Fuentes' *corridos* were published in *El Grito* Vol. 6 (Spring, 1973): 3-40. His "Soy Chicano" and "Corrido de César Chávez" were recorded by Arhoolie (45-529B) in 1975. In 1970 the Teatro Chicano de Austin recorded his "Soy tu Hermano" and "Mexico-Americano" to be sold at *teatro* performances. The five hundred copies were all sold and never re-

recorded by them. However, Arhoolie recorded "Mexico-Americano" on its album, *Music of la Raza* Vol. 1 (3002).

¹⁷A detailed review of *La Gran Carpa* is included in Kourilsky, "Approaching Quetzalcoatl," pp. 44-46.

¹⁸Teatro Chicano de Austin, "Las Avispas," *Revista Chicano-Riqueña* Vol. 2 (Summer, 1974): 8-10.

¹⁹The most accepted term for the Mexican American dialect of Spanish is *caló*. See George R. Alvarez, "Caló: the 'Other Spanish,' " *Etc. a Review of General Semantics* 34 (March, 1967): 7-13.

²⁰". . . and from that time on that border just south of us has existed. Sure, but it's a very capricious border, not recognized by Mexican workers. And if somebody has the nerve to call me a wetback just because I crossed a little river just so wide, he better find out who's the super-wetback who crossed that great ocean to get here. Yes, sir, because I came to this land. But I was also born in this land. That's why I've come to tell you this story, the story about the *migra* (The Immigration and Naturalization Service). Yes, sir, that snake, that animal that's putting it to our mother (literally, "Mexico," figuratively "fucking our mothers"). The story begins in 1970 when all of a sudden: Watch out, here comes the *migra!*"

²¹See my review of this festival, "Séptimo Festival de los Teatros," *Latin American Theater Review* 10 (Fall, 1976).

²²For a brief history of El Teatro de la Esperanza, see Jorge Huerta, "Concerning Teatro Chicano," pp. 18-20.

²³Guillermo Loo, "Editorial," *El Boletín Cultural de TENAZ* 1 (1976): 1-2.

# Chicano Theater:
# A Popular Culture Battleground

Chicano theater is closer to the pulse and heartbeat of working class Mexican Americans than any other art form or communications medium. Its development is closely linked to the various social and political struggles of the people of Mexican descent in the United States: among others, the farmworkers' efforts to organize agricultural labor unions, the working class parents' attempts to make the schools responsive to their childrens' linguistic and cultural needs, the Chicano students' movement to forge an identity and lead the American civil rights battle. *Teatro Chicano* has at each step served as a vehicle for sensitizing Mexican American communities and involving them in these and other struggles for their socio-political needs, their cultural identity and their movement strategies. In the eleven years since Luis Valdez founded the Teatro Campesino[1] to propagandize the farmworkers' strike in Delano, California, this basic link of a people's theater with a labor or social movement has been duplicated from coast to coast. The Teatro de la Gente and the cannery workers in San Jose, the Teatro Alma Latina and the Puerto Rican tomato pickers in South Jersey, the Teatro Trucha and the St. Luke's hospital workers in Chicago are but three of the over one hundred such groups now operating throughout the country.

While using the basic dramatic format created by the Teatro Campesino, each theater in its own way reflects the total cultural and socio-political makeup of its community. The work of the individual Chicano theater basically consists of the motivation of its community audiences to carry on the movement for a Mexican or Chicano cultural identity in the face of attempted homogenization by the dominant Anglo-American culture. Not only is Chicano theater a Mexican American popular culture medium, then, but it is also a battleground for Mexican cultural integrity as challenged by American popular culture. In answer to the English language and the American Dream, Chicano theater proffers the Spanish language and a host of Mexican values, customs and myths. The popular media's stereotype of Mexicans as lazy, fat bandits, for example, is countered by the theater's stereotypes of Anglo-Americans and by the dynamism of such folk heroes as Emiliano Zapata, Francisco Villa and César Chávez. The ever-present popularized history surrounding the Davy Crocketts and Sam Houstons is debunked by the re-writing of the conquest of the Southwest on the Chicano stages. For every hamburger there is a taco, for every John Wayne a Tony Aguilar, for every John Denver hit a *corrido*, for every nostalgic item in the Anglo popular mentality a Mexican American counterpart.

The basic unit of Chicano theater is the *acto*, a short, satirical sketch designed to "Inspire the audience to social action. Illuminate specific points about social problems. Show or hint at solution. Express what people are feeling."[2] The *acto* was developed by Luis Valdez and the Teatro Campesino in 1965 and was quickly adopted by Chicano theaters that were emerging everywhere. *Actos* are the theatrical weapons that Chicanos use to challenge the stereotypes that are promoted in the popular media. *Actos*, in response to these stereotypes, promote a positive Mexican American or Chicano identity. They do so by questioning the credibility of the American Dream and by re-enforcing Mexican American popular culture. And the Mexican American popular culture that is advanced by *teatros* includes popular dialects of Spanish, popular and folk music, folk heroes, traditional foods and numerous cultural alternatives to the established "American way." In many cases, out and out warfare between the two systems of existence takes place on the Chicano stages.

Basically a propagandistic and agitational dramatic instrument, the *acto* is related to various types of Mexican folk theater.[3] Nevertheless, the *acto* has received the influence of *the* propagandistic dramatic sketch par excellence, the television commercial. Not only do Chicano theaters at times borrow promotional techniques from television, but they also succeed in turning the television commercials against themselves. Commercials that denigrate Mexican identity or shrewdly exploit Anglo-American identity are inverted by *teatros*. The Frito Bandito, the Clairol Lady, the Mexican in the Marlboro commercial have all suffered this fate.

A typical treatment is that accorded to the Radio Free Europe commercial that features a blank-eyed child with a padlock and chain on his head and being brainwashed by messages through a blaring loudspeaker. The Teatro Chicano de Austin usurped the commercial's basic dramatic structure and inverted its message by showing three Chicano children being brainwashed in American schools by two militaristic, drill instructor-teachers. The three zombie-like children with padlocks and chains on their heads mechanically repeat the following statements dictated to them by the teachers: "All good Americans speak English. César Chávez is a commie. Lettuce each day keeps the doctor away. Mexicans are thugs and Pachucos. Mexicans should work in the fields because they are built close to the ground. White is right. Blonds have more fun."[4] After this brainwashing, the children and teachers rise to attention as another character appears and addresses the audience: "There are over fifteen million Chicanos in the United States. First they stole our land and now they want to steal our minds."

Another *acto* that borrows heavily from television commercials is *Man From Huelga* (strike), which is inspired in the Glad-Wrap commercial. The *acto*, performed by the Teatro de Ustedes from Denver, El Teatro de la Revolución from Greeley and many others, depicts a family sitting down to a lunch that includes boycotted lettuce, Gallo wine and Coors beer. An argument ensues when one of the characters tries to persuade the others to stop consuming the boycotted products. From backstage someone shouts, "Man from Huelga, Man from Huelga, trouble brewing at the Romero residence," whereupon the Man from Huelga appears attired in a Superman-type outfit and delivers the following statement:

> I am the Man from Huelga. And I would like to let you know that the basis of this argument is because you don't know why the boycott is happening. You, with that iceberg head lettuce, didn't you know that the United Farmworkers are struggling for better wages, for better working conditions, and the right to their own union? Get rid of that lettuce and try some leaf lettuce. The audacity to drink that Coors beer when Coors has been dumping waste in the gulches and has destroyed acres of potato fields in the San Luis Valley with its weather modification.

You should be ashamed of yourself, young lady. And you with the Gallo wine, the same struggle as with the lettuce. Don't you know there's blood on them grapes!

Here the "Man from Glad" commercial, itself inspired by characters like Superman and the Man from U.N.C.L.E., has been transformed into a propagandistic vehicle for workers' strikes and boycotts.

*Teatros* will most often perform bilingually, although they may perform solely in English or Spanish under certain circumstances. Chicano theaters address their linguistically heterogeneous audiences by continuously switching from English to Spanish, as is common in every day speech in the *barrios*. Furthermore, *teatros* employ common dialects of Spanish and English, but often exhibit a particular predilection for the use of *caló*,[5] an argot commonly used by young Chicanos throughout the Southwest. Besides maintaining the tension between English and Spanish in their own theatrical language, the *teatros* depict in their scenes the common language conflicts that Chicanos experience in dealing with the society's public institutions: schools, hospitals, welfare departments, etc.

In some Southwestern states, for instance, speaking Spanish on school grounds was prohibited to Mexican American children. The linguistic conflict that this has caused has been dramatized in such *actos* as *Escuela* (School), performed by the Teatro Chicano de Austin, the Teatro Desengaño del Pueblo from Gary, and the Teatro del Piojo from Seattle. The *acto* is set on the first day of school in a kindergarten whose enrollment is mainly Chicano. Upon realizing that his students speak only Spanish, the teacher immediately admonishes, "You are in the United States now. And in the United States *everybody* speaks English. And in the United States *everyone* has an American name. So if your name is Juan, why we change that to John. Or if your name is Ricardo, well that becomes Richard, you see." He then proceeds to change each child's name: Juan Paniaguas to John Bread and Water, María Dolores de la Barriga to Mary Stomach Pains, Casimiro Flores to I Almost See Flowers, and Domingo Nieves to Ice Cream Sunday. The *acto* continues with a series of humorous misinterpretations and reaches its climax when Ice Cream Sunday urinates in his pants because the teacher refuses to find out what his needs are, unless he expresses them in English.

Like hundreds of other *actos, Escuela* gives its audiences some insights into the failings of American society to live up to the egalitarian ideals that constitute its political identity. *Escuela* depicts American xenophobia and discrimination in the form of the teacher rejecting the Chicano children's food and clothing and checking them over for lice. But American society receives an even more direct indictment in works like *The American Dream*, by Chicago's Teatro del Barrio, and *El Corrido de Juan Endrogado*, by San Jose's Teatro de la Gente. Both works attack the commonly held beliefs that constitute the American Dream: opportunity, freedom and equality.

*The American Dream* is a modern allegory that features the American Dream as a central character. She is the Statue of Liberty draped in an American flag and emerges from a long line of flag-waving, death-masked, allegorical figures that represent America in *teatro*. In this *acto* a Mexican American searches for his identity in this land of plenty. He becomes associated with other Americans who are also searching for theirs. When with Blacks he is pursued by the Ku Klux Klan. With the hippies he is beaten by the Chicago police. Finally his odyssey takes him into military service where he is given a one-way ticket to Vietnam and death. Throughout the *acto*, the American Dream manipulates the action while deriving immense pleasure from observing the misfortunes of the Mexican American.

*El Corrido de Juan Endrogado*, written by El Teatro de la Gente's Adrián Vargas, deals with the addiction of poor people to the attractive material symbols of success that the American Dream dangles before the eyes of poor people. The main character, Juan Endrogado (John Drugged), is a down-and-out Mexican American who looks for work in vain. He feels the need for the big and powerful cars, the fast women and the high paying jobs that are indexes of success in this society. But he only obtains his dreams through the stupor of drugs. In *Juan Endrogado*, Vargas has merged the world of sexual fantasy with the consumer ethic in his two characters, Chevy Impala and K-Mart, two prostitutes that approach Juan:

American Dream: Say there, boy, I can see that you're looking for the life America has to offer. Well, I'm that American Dream pimp . . . I can turn you on to any one of these divine symbols of American progress. Now don't say nothing before you have a chance to meet each one and make up your mind. (The Chevrolet theme song is played in the background.)

Chevy: Hi there, honey, my name is Impala and you can drive me anywhere you want to. Dig my sleek body lines and style. Performance? Oh, baby, you'll just love the way I handle! A strong man needs something fast, something he can feel powerful with. I'm it, baby. How about taking me for a ride?

Juan: Well, I can dig it, honey. But you look too expensive for me.

Narrator-Singer (singing): Put on your fine threads, Johnny, 'cause we're going out tonight. Put on your red dress, baby, 'cause we're going out tonight.

K-Mart: Hey, Johnny, how about trying me on for size? I'm not as expensive as she is, but I can still show you a good time.

Johnny: All right!

K-Mart: We'll sit together and drink our Gallo wine. You'll look very impressive with me around. I'll clothe you with my colorful personality. And, you know what they say, clothes make the man.

Johnny: Well, hey baby, what's your name?

K-Mart: Well, some call me Macy's, others call me Emporium, but you can call me K-Mart.

Johnny: Well . . . uh . . . (Both prostitutes begin to fight over him.) Wait a minute, wait a minute! To tell you the truth, I can't afford either of you. I'm broke.

Chevy and K-Mart: Broke?!!

A third lady of the night, however, wins out over the other two that Juan cannot afford. She is Hunger, who later converts to Death. Thus we can see how in *El Corrido de Juan Endrogado* American status symbols and materialistic consumption in the guise of Chevy Impala, K-Mart, Macy's and Emporium are satirized. The alternative given by the *acto* to the onslaught of this addiction to American materialism is the unity of the Chicano family. In the end, Juan's family succors him and Death is turned against the system: the pimp and the two prostitutes.

Closely related to these visions of the American Dream are Chicano theater's demythologizing of American history, especially the popular version of "how the West was won." Contemporary Chicano identity takes as its critical origin the Mexican-American War and the incorporation of previously owned Mexican lands into the American nation. The stigma of being a conquered and colonized people has afflicted Mexican Americans throughout this century. It should be no surprise, therefore, that the Chicano theaters in the Southwest try to penetrate the layers of mythology that fill the textbooks, movies and television programs concerned with the "opening of the West." Historic shrines like the Alamo, toponyms like Austin and Houston, movies and television programs based on the life and legend of figures like Davy Crockett are ever-present reminders of the defeat, colonization and anti-Mexicanism that has in part shaped Chicano identity. But the Chicano theaters are not so much concerned with rewriting the official history of the Southwest as in combating the popular myths that have arisen from political and racist motives. Beside the image of the fearless Texas Ranger stands the image of the cowardly and treacherous Mexican in the popular mentality. To be raised under the influence of these stigmas is powerfully demoralizing and must be seen as partially responsible for contemporary Chicano social and political reactions.

Quite reasonably, Chicano theaters in Austin and San Antonio, the historic seats of Texas fervor and anti-Mexicanism, were among the first to re-examine the Texas Revolution on stage. In *Papá México*, the Teatro Chicano de Austin conceptualized Old Mexico as the loving father of five daughters: California, New Mexico, Arizona, Colorado and Texas. Father Mexico befriends "the first wetback in history," Stephen F. Austin, who manages to cross the Mississippi into Mexico looking for land and opportunity. Austin pays Mexico back for his kindness by calling over a couple of drunken friends, Sam Houston and Kit Carson, who join him later in stabbing Father Mexico in the back and raping his daughters. In another *acto, High School*, the Teatro Chicano de Austin portrayed high schoolers correcting their teacher's misconceptions and prejudices by pointing out that the Texas Revolution was a rebellion of both Anglo and Mexican residents of Texas against the central government of Mexico. They argue that there were Mexicans who died defending the Alamo and that a Mexican, Lorenzo de Zavala, was the first Vice President of the Texas Republic.

The Teatro de los Barrios came out from beneath the shadow of the historic Alamo, the perennial symbol of Anglo-Texan glory and Mexican humiliation, to write and perform their *El Alamo* in 1973. Héctor F. González, the director and author of the play, explains the reasons for creating the work:

> This work was written because for many years in the United States we have been taught a biased history. We have always been taught that the Mexicans were assassins; later we were converted to cowards, liars, and lazy people.
>
> These are the descriptions that the Gringo uses when discriminating against Mexicans. That is why we Chicanos also suffer at the hands of the Gringo oppressor. In school they always teach us that Davy Crockett died gallantly and that he was a superman too great for the Mexicans (like John Wayne killing many Mexicans single handedly). But in truth, those heroes of the Alamo were made of flesh and blood just like anyone else. They never talk about or show the racism that existed in the mentality of the men of the Alamo. Nor do they talk about how they were just interested in Mexico and Texas for their riches.

The history of the Alamo is always seen as an act of democracy and morality. They say that the Gringos went to free Texas from the tyrannous hands of Santa Ana. They never explain that Mexico had no way of maintaining Texas or that Mexico did not allow slavery. But the streets of Washington, D.C., the capital of the United States, ran red with the blood of chained slaves. Neither do they explain that Mexico only allowed them to enter Texas without slaves and that Mexico gave them plenty of land without telling them that the lands belonged to the Indians. The Gringos only came to make Texas another slave state for the union.

We, the Mexicans and Chicanos, have suffered because of these prejudices in the schools (they say we are assassins), at work (because we are inferior; there were two hundred fifty Gringos against thousands of Mexicans at the Alamo), and in the economy (because the Gringos stole our ancestors' lands and riches).

This is why this play was written: to tell everyone about the other side of what happened at the Alamo. And this is closer to the truth of what happened at the Alamo.[6]

*El Alamo* goes beyond demythologizing the figures of Davy Crockett, James Bowie and William Barret Travis. It consciously exploits the shock value of discrediting the hallowed personages of the Texan Pantheon. Crockett is portrayed as a political opportunist who wanted to use Texas as a stepping stone in his career. Crockett, the fierce Indian fighter, introduces himself with the following: "I'm Davy Crockett from Tennessee. When I fought against the Injuns in Florida I ate fried tators, fried in Injun flesh. Yes sir, I'm as strong as a bear! And I hates INJUNS!" James Bowie, who supposedly killed fifty men with his famed knife, introduces himself in the following manner: "I'm from Kentucky. I was a gambler and I had lots of money, *dinero*! Then in Galveston, Texas, I sold blackies (slaves) with false papers to a pirate. Then in Kansas I sold land with false papers to rob people. Things were getting hot in Kansas . . . (Someone yells "Silver mines found in Texas!") I guess I'll go to Texas and make me some money." Worst of all,

Travis is accused of having killed a man in South Carolina and of having shifted the blame to his slave. Thereafter he escaped to Texas to avoid further repercussions from the killing. It is also insinuated in the play that Travis committed suicide at the Alamo instead of fighting to the death.

The Mexicans, on the other hand, are no longer shown as cruel and inhumane, but as hungry, poorly clad and forcefully conscripted against their will. The Mexican army is depicted as suffering from a lack of finances, poor organization and low morale. Moreover, the play emphasizes the opportunities given to the Texans to surrender and leave Texas without bloodshed. It is pointed out later, however, that Houston did not give the Mexican army at San Jacinto the same chance that Santa Ana gave the Texans. As can be seen in *El Alamo* and in other historical *actos*, Chicano theaters at times counter Anglo distortions of Mexican history and culture with some distortions and exaggerations of their own.

The national bicentennial celebration afforded Chicano theaters an even greater opportunity for expressing their version of American history. Throughout the year, the nation was subjected to a flood of popularized history over the air waves and a romanticized and chauvinistic vision of the making of this nation. The national Chicano theater organization, TENAZ, (Teatro Nacional de Aztlán), thus decided to sponsor four festivals at separate sites throughout the West to counteract the impact of patriotic commercialism and media saturation. The festivals were held in Seattle (June 24 to July 4), Denver (July 10 to July 17), San Jose (August 6 to August 8) and Los Angeles (August 22 to August 29) to expose as many people as possible to the Chicano's vision of the other side of American history. Of the many *actos* that focused on the bicentennial, two of the most interesting from a popular culture standpoint were the Teatro Urbano's *Anti-bicentennial Special* and Teatro Desengaño del Pueblo's *Bicentennial*.

The *Anti-Bicentennial Special*, by Los Angeles' Teatro Urbano, is a zany burlesque on popular figures like Uncle Sam, George Washington, Betsy Ross, Benjamin Franklin, Abraham Lincoln and George Armstrong Custer. The piece is performed to a sound-track made up of World War II movie songs a la Dick Powell and George M. Cohan. The heavily made-up and masked characters each present a monolog through which is seen their failure to live up to the glorious ideals behind the founding of this nation. Of course, Custer's inhumanity toward the Indians and George Washington's ownership of slaves are highlighted, but figures like Betsy Ross are used to call attention to women's inequality throughout the history of this country. The whole affair is performed in front of a ten-foot high American flag as backdrop.

*Bicentennial*, created by the younger members (ages six to fifteen) of the Teatro Desengaño del Pueblo from Gary, is a thoroughly sophisticated attack on the commercialism and chauvinism that characterized the bicentennial celebration. The characters make their entrance in a parade, singing the jingle from the Yankee Doodle fast food commercials: "It's a Yankee Doodle Dandy day, a Yankee Doodle Dandy day. Come on down where the good times are. Yankee Doodle Dandy. Yankee Doodle Dandy." An announcer explains that they are going to celebrate the bicentennial with the presentation of historic figures from the American Revolution. The first actor is supposed to do an impression of Paul Revere but mistakenly does one of the popular rock and roll group, Paul Revere and the Raiders. Next, John Hancock is shown signing the Declaration of Independence. But immediately after this act, the announcer begins to auction off to the audience the Declaration of Independence, John Hancock's plumed pen, his tennis shoes, a lock of his hair and even John Hancock himself. But the *coup de grace* is the presentation of this conversation between Betsy Ross and George Washington:

Betsy: I'm almost done with your flag, George.

George: What do I want a flag for? I want guns.

Betsy: Guns? What do you want guns for?

George: So I can shoot some cans, of course.

Betsy: Cans? What kinds of cans?

George: Some Mexi*cans*, some Puerto Ri*cans* and some Afri*cans*.

Betsy (admiringly): Oh, George, you're so violent!

Although Chicanos have been left out of American history textbooks and classes, the bicentennial celebration has helped to alienate them even more clearly they are not without history or tradition. Chicano theaters have reconstructed a Mexican people's history for themselves. It is an alternative to the formalized history of colonization and exploitation. The *teatro*'s version of Mexican-Chicano history begins in pre-Columbian Mexico and tells of the birth of the *mestizo* and his endurance and survival in the face of wars with European powers, revolutions and mass migrations of epic proportions. This tale of the Chicanos is that of the children of the earth and the sun, the Indian converts to Christianity through the miracle of Our Lady of Guadalupe, the rebellious followers of Hidalgo, Zapata and now Chávez, and the millions of Mexican American workers who trace their ancestry to the Aztecs, their language to the Spaniards and their livelihood to the United States.

At the fifth annual Chicano theater festival, held in Mexico City in 1974, Chicano identification with Aztec and Mayan roots came to a head with the festival's overriding theme being the Chicano's return to his pre-Columbian origins.[7] Quite fittingly, the opening ceremonies and the first performances were held at the foot of the Pyramid of the Sun at Teotihuacan, and numerous *teatros* had specially prepared for the occasion *mitos* or dramatizations of Aztec and Mayan myths with relevance to contemporary life. The festival also fostered a massive exchange among more than forty Latin American theaters and thus solidified the Chicano's relationship, not only with the indigenous cultural past, but also with contemporary Latin America.

Repeatedly the *mitos* examined life before the coming of the Spaniards and then explored the all-important act, the birth of the *mestizo*. Often recalling Malinche's illicit relationship with Cortez, at times depicting Spaniards raping Aztec women, each *teatro* concurred in envisioning the birth as a tremendous trauma. Some *teatros*, like El Teatro Campesino, were somewhat more esoteric in their presentations by delving into the mysteries of Mayan cosmology with their *Baile de los Gigantes* (The Dance of the Giants). Others were more practical. El Teatro de la Gente, for example, applied the myth of Quetzalcoatl to U.S. imperialism and even cast Coca-Cola as one of the villainous characters in the myth. But the *acto* that best completes the picture of the Chicano theaters' view of history is Teatro Campesino's *La Gran Carpa de la Familia Rascuachi* (The Tent of the Underdogs), for it fully integrates the cultural past with the contemporary development of the Chicano. The *Gran Carpa* does consider the birth of the *mestizo*, as well as the miraculous apparition of Our Lady of Guadalupe to Juan Diego. But it also deals with the experiences of Chicanos in the United States by following three generations of the Pelado (naked, poor) family through migration, farmwork, children, Vietnam and a complete series of archetypal experiences.

But Chicano history as seen by the *teatros* is not only a recounting of the pre-Columbian cultural past and the trials and tribulations of the Mexican American workers, like Jesus Pelado in the *Gran Carpa*. It also sings in praise of the people's victories and of their heroes: Emiliano Zapata, Francisco Villa, César Chávez and others. While Chicano theaters have attacked the mythology surrounding popular, anti-Mexican American heroes, they have at the same time augmented the folk traditions surrounding such figures as Zapata, Villa and other historical and contemporary personages. One of the primary vehicles for the continuation of this tradition has been the *corrido* or ballad that recounts the adventures of these larger than life figures. But of even greater importance for Chicano theaters has been the continuation of the *corridos fronterizos* or border ballads that deal with the conflict of Anglos and Mexicans along the Southwestern frontier with Mexico. Many of the heroes of these Mexican ballads are considered by the Chicano theaters to be social bandits or primitive revolutionaries. And in these *corridos* the Mexican "bandits," such as Juan Nepomuceno Cortina, Gregorio Cortez, Jacinto Treviño and Joaquín Murieta,[8] almost always emerge victorious from their clashes with the Anglo establishment.

Among the many *teatros* that have dramatized these *corridos* is the Teatro Chicano de Austin with its version of the *Corrido de Jacinto Treviño*. The cowardly Texas Rangers, depicted as mongrels trained to protect the interests of Anglo ranchers who have stolen Mexican lands, are humiliated and killed by the daring Jacinto Treviño. Both the original *corrido* itself and the *acto* embody the type of culture clash that results in the dehumanization of both Anglos and Mexicans, although the sense of an epic struggle between two peoples is still conveyed through this type of heroic balladry and drama. But Teatro Chicano de Austin has presented an even more vivid portrayal of the sanguinary strife between Anglos and Mexicans in their singing of one of the oldest extant *corridos*, *El Corrido de Joaquín Murieta*:

Yo no soy americano
pero comprendo el inglés.
Me lo aprendí de mi hermano
al derecho y al revés.
A cualquier americano
lo hago temblar a mis pies.

Cuando apenas era un niño
huérfano a mí me dejaron.
Sin que me hiciera un cariño
a mi hermano lo colgaron.
A su esposa Carmelita
cobardes la asesinaron.

No soy chileno ni extraño
en este suelo en que piso.
De México es California
porque Dios así lo quiso.
En mi sarape cosido
traigo mi fe de bautizo.

Yo me vine de Hermosillo
en busca de oro y riqueza.
Al indio noble y sencillo
lo defendí con fiereza.
El gobierno americano
puso precio en mi cabeza.

Yo me metía en cantinas
castigando americanos.

"Tú serás el capitán,
el que mataste a mi hermano.
Lo agarraste indefenso,
miserable americano."

Yo me pase a California
como el año de cincuenta
en mi montura plateada
y mi pistola repleta.
Yo soy ese mexicano.
Mi nombre es Joaquín Murieta.

(I am not an American
but I understand English.
My brother and I learned it
backwards and forwards.
I make any American
tremble at my feet.

(When I was but a child
they left me orphaned.
Without ever letting him caress me
they hung my brother dead
and as for his wife Carmelita,
the cowards killed her too.

(I am not a Chilean nor a foreigner
on the soil that I stand.
To Mexico belongs California.
God willed it that way.
In my hand-sewn sarape
I carry my faith since baptism.

(I came from Hermosillo
looking for gold and riches.
Then I fiercely defended
the noble and simple Indian.
The American government

put a price on my head.

(I would go into cantinas
to punish Americans.
"You must be that captain,
the one who killed my brother.
You took him defenseless,
you lowly American.

(I came to California
about the year eighteen fifty
riding a silver studded mount
and carrying a loaded pistol.
I am that Mexican.
My name is Joaquín Murieta.)

The culture conflict that is part and parcel of Chicano theater is also an indication of the interior psychological conflict of Chicanos who are increasingly faced with the decisions of accepting an "American" lifestyle or carrying on traditional Mexican behavior patterns. Young Chicanos often feel they must choose to speak English or Spanish, living in the suburban melting pot or in the *barrio*, and even between such seemingly insignificant things as eating a hamburger[8] or a taco. In most cases the conflict is resolved by choosing a biculturalism that permits both modes of behavior where possible. This is the true meaning of Chicanismo. Often *teatros* have not emphasized this enough, opting to over-protect the Mexican side of their cultural heritage because of the real dangers of acculturation and assimilation. "México Americano," a song composed by Rumel Fuentes, former member of the Teatro Chicano de Austin, is one of the few cultural statements in *teatro* that asserts this dual allegiance:

Por mi madre yo soy mexicano.
Por destino soy americano.
Yo soy de la raza de oro.
Yo soy méxico americano.

Yo te comprendo el inglés.

También te hablo el castellano.
Yo soy de la raza noble.
Yo soy méxico americano.

Zacatecas a Minnesota,
de Tijuana a Nueva York,
dos países son mi tierra.
Los defiendo con mi honor.

Dos idiomas y dos países,
dos culturas tengo yo.
Es mi suerte y tengo orgullo
porque así lo mando Dios.

(Mexican by parentage,
American by destiny,
I am of the golden race.
I am Mexican American.

(I know the English language.
I also speak Spanish.
I am of the noble race.
I am Mexican American.

(Zacatecas to Minnesota,
from Tijuana to New York,
two countries have I.
I'll defend them with my honor.

(Two languages and two countries,
two cultures are mine.
It's my fate and I'm proud,
for it's the will of God.)

As we have seen throughout this study, Chicano theatre has functioned as a Mexican American popular culture medium that attempts to reenforce the survival of a Mexican or Chicano identity in the face of the threat of Anglo-American cultural domination.

*Teatro* has been in the forefront of Chicano political and cultural movements at all times, and in so doing it has been a combative weapon attacking stereotypes of Mexicans, countering popularized anti-Mexican American history, and satirizing those facets of the American Dream that have been false promises to poor people and that function to obliterate a people's ethnic identity.

On the other hand, Chicano theaters have reconstructed and popularized their own Mexican-Chicano history as an alternative of "American" history for Chicanos: a proud indigenous past, the survival and adaptation of the *mestizo*, and the people's victories and folk heroes in Mexico and the United States. It is also evident that the culture conflict that *teatros* exhibit is the result of the long history of real life warfare, discrimination and misunderstanding. Only rarely do *teatros* succeed in demonstrating a true resolution to the cultural conflict that has had deep psychological repercussions on the individual. That song "Mexico Americano" is one of the few *teatro* statements that affirm a pride and confidence in Chicano biculturalism by emphasizing an American as well as a Mexican heritage.

[1]For a short history of the Teatro Campesino, see Francoise Kourilsky, "Approaching Quetzalcoatl. The Evolution of El Teatro Campesino," *Performance*, 7 (Fall, 1973),37-46, and for a longer, in-depth treatment, see Jorge A. Huerta, *Chicano Theatre. Themes and Forms* (Ypsilanti: Bilingual Press, 1982).

[2]*Actos by Luis Valdez y el Teatro Campesino.* (Fresno: Cucaracha Press, 1971), p.8.

[3]See my article "Elementos hispánicos en el teatro chicano," *Actas del XVI Congreso del Instituto Internacional de Literatura Iberoamericana* (Madrid: Centro Iberoamericano de Cooperación, 1978).

[4]Most of the *actos* quoted in my text have not been published. My data are the result of eight years of personal experience as an actor-director in *teatro*. During the last few years I have been taping and photographing *teatros* throughout the country. Thus the quotes are from my recordings.

[5]See George C. Barker, "Pachuco: An American Spanish Argot and Its Social Function in Tucson, Arizona," *El Lenguaje de los Chicanos, Regional and Social Characteristics of Language used by Mexican Americans*, eds. Eduardo Hernandez Chavez, Andrew D. Cohen and Anthony F. Beltramo (Arlington: Center for Applied Linguistics, 1975), 183-201.

[6]This is my translation of the introduction from the unpublished manuscript of *El Alamo*.

[7]See Theodore Shank, "A Return to Mayan and Aztec Roots," *The Drama Review*, 18 (Dec., 1974), 56-70.

[8]See Mody C. Boatright, ed., *Mexican Border Ballads* (Dallas: Southwestern University Press, 1967); Vicente T. Mendoza, *El Romance y el Corrido Mexicano* (Mexico, 1939); Américo Paredes, *A Texas-Mexican Cancionero: Folksongs of the Lower Border* (Urbana: University of Illinois Press, 1976).

[9]San Diego's Teatro Mostizo has a comic take-off on Jack-in-the-Box hamburgers in their *Los Cuatro Años de Colegio* (The Four Years of College). Part of their satire is a change in the lyrics of the Jack-in-the-Box jingle:

| | |
|---|---|
| Well, come eat some shit, | Come eat some shit, |
| hamburger waste, | hamburger waste, |
| at Jack-in-the-Box. | at Jack-in-the-Box. |
| Come on you Spics, | Come on you Spics, |
| Niggers and Chinks | Niggers and Chinks |
| to Jack-in-the-Box. | to Jack-in-the-Box. |
| Our food is really heavy. | |
| We don't care | Watch out McDonalds! |
| 'cause we'll be wealthier. | (spoken) |

# Fifty Years of Theater in the Latino Communities of Northwest Indiana

Over the last fifty years, northwest Indiana has attracted settlement by Spanish-speaking peoples. Dating from the second decade of the twentieth century, the urban, industrial complexes of Gary and East Chicago received large-scale immigration from Mexico and migration from the Southwest. The influx of Mexicans was curtailed during the depression years only to be re-established after World War II. But postwar immigration was also accompanied by migration to the area of another Spanish-speaking group, the Puerto Ricans. The Spanish-speaking inhabitants of the area were quick to establish a rich community life, one that depended on various communications media, such as newspapers, radio and, later, television programs, as well as leisure-time activities: sports, festivals, dances, etc. As far as community art, entertainment and ritual are concerned, one institution stands out above all others—community theater. Drama is the most social of community art forms and, therefore, the most indicative of the growth of the community, its changes in attitudes and identity. The following is a brief survey of Gary and East Chicago (earlier Indiana Harbor) theater groups, plays and performances. May it contribute to the study of these communities' preservation of their ethnic and religious identity.

By the 1920's, at least five theater groups were operating in Gary and the Indiana Harbor section of East Chicago: Cuadro de Aficionados de Gary, the Arcos Family, the Cuadro of the Cruz Azul Mexicana Benefit Society and the Cuadro Dramático del Círculo de Obreros Católicos "San José."[1] In addition to the performances of these community groups, both cities also hosted professional theater companies and vaudevillians presenting *cuadros de variedades, zarzuelas, sainetes* and even operettas. Most of these groups, and those that follow, were closely tied to two central institutions in the Mexican community: the church and the mutual aid society. Of the three or four societies sponsoring plays during the 1920's, the one which had the greatest success and existed for the longest time was also the one that was most closely tied to the church; in this case, it was Our Lady of Guadalupe Church in Indiana Harbor. The Círculo de Obreros Católicos "San José" was founded on April 12, 1925, for the purposes of: (1) raising funds for the construction of a church; (2) promoting the welfare of fellow Mexicans and working for the education of their children; (3) raising funds for a library; and (4) providing wholesome forms of recreation for the members.[3] The Círculo created the Cuadro Dramático to provide this "wholesome recreation" and raise funds for the construction of Our Lady of Guadalupe Church.

Nine plays were produced by the Cuadro Dramático from March, 1927 until May, 1928.[4] Community involvement in the productions was extensive and included participation for actors in casts often in excess of twenty characters, in addition to promptors, scenographers, musicians, ushers, etc. Moreover, judging from the records of ticket sales, the productions drew audiences of over two hundred people. Along with the aficionados who produced these plays, former professional theatrical people such as J. Jesús Cabrera took part. After interrupting his directing career in Mexico City to take refuge in Indiana Harbor from the Mexican Revolution, he directed all of the plays of the Cuadro Dramático and also provided the group with its scripts.[5] This explains why most of the plays produced by the Cuadro were still being performed in Mexico City.[6]

The Great Depression and the mass repatriation of Mexicans from the area eventually put an end to the Cuadro Dramático's activities, as well as the activities of the other groups. Immediately following the advent of the economic cataclysm, J. Jesús Cabrera returned to Mexico where he later died. Not until the sixties was there any real regeneration of dramatic activity in these communities.[7]

Only spotty information on church-related dramatic productions of the 1950's has been preserved.[8] Interviews and examination of church documents reveal only irregular performances of Christmas plays and plays on the Guadalupe theme, most noteworthy of which was the *Aparición de la Virgen de Guadalupe*, produced in 1954, to celebrate the silver jubilee of the founding of East Chicago's Our Lady of Guadalupe Church. In typical fashion, for the occasion, the text of the play was obtained in book form from Mexico by Sister Cordelia Marie.[9] It seems that the parishioners who performed the play had no intention of continuing their theatrical avocation; as most often happened with such commemorative, religious productions, communal religious celebration rather than interest in drama was primary.

Perhaps a sign that the Mexican community of East Chicago was once again back on its feet and healthy was the abundant theatrical activity, of a more serious nature, that took place during the 1960's. Besides the more ephemeral dramatic productions like the *Cuadro de Navidad* presented at the Texas Club in 1962,[10] and *The Life, Passion and Death of Jesus Christ* at the Unión Benéfica Mexicana (UBM) in 1963,[11] two important drama associations have left a record of productivity during this period: El Teatro Experimental Talía and El Club Artístico Guadalupano. The first of these groups was founded in conjunction with the Unión Benéfica Mexicana by theater aficionados who had previously taken part in dramatizations at the club.[12] Gildardo Peral, who has since become president of the UBM, and Vicente Osvaldo Valjaló, a Chilean who had directed *El Milagro del Tepeyac*, founded Talía to enrich artistic pursuits in the community, even though the participants, who had for the most part no previous experience in theater, included secretaries, nurses, machine operators, electricians and painters.[13] Their first and last production, *Honrarás a tu Madre*, by the Argentine writer Mario Chismaro, was executed on May 7 and 14, 1961, at the Unión Benéfica Mexicana in conjunction with the club's Mother's Day festivities.[14] On October 27, 1961, the *Latin Times* announced in an article under the headline of "Por Ultima Vez," the last performance of the play on October 27, in a program that was to last more than three hours, including a "fin de fiesta" of songs, poetry recitation, *ballet folklórico* and speeches. After this one last performance, the Teatro Experimental Experimental Talía was never heard from again.

The Club Artístico Guadalupano, whose constitution dates from 1961, was to exist for over a decade, during which time it was to serve not only as a source of dramatic productions, but also as an association of talented people who could enrich any community affair with cultural presentations and speeches. Initiated on an informal basis in the late fifties, by the time the club's constitution was signed, the membership included nineteen men who periodically affirmed through a formal oath their loyalty to the principles of the constitution which included the following objectives:

1. Ayudar a través de presentaciones artísticas morales, a la elevación cultural, moral, educativa y espiritual de la sociedad en general.
2. Organizar toda clase de eventos culturales con el firme propósito de interesar a la juventud a tomar parte activa, ayudando así a retirarla del ocio y la vagancia, que dañan y desequilibran el carácter del joven.
3. Adquirir, de acuerdo con los medios económicos al alcance del club, diferentes juegos de mesa, artículos propios para la formación de un gimnasio y administrarlo debidamente, ofreciendo de esta manera un lugar donde la juventud reciba una educación física de acuerdo con sus habilidades.
4. Formar y organizar una biblioteca para que los miembros hagan uso de ella, y otras personas que lo deseen, . . . pero siempre y cuando el cuerpo administrativo del club lo autorice. No se permitirá por ningún motivo que figuren volúmenes de obras inmorales ni libros escritos con tendencias comunistas o de autores así declarados.
5. Cooperar con las demás organizaciones parroquiales, y si se es posible, con otras que soliciten la cooperación del club.
6. Extender la ayuda a las personas en desgracia cuando a criterio de la membresía se crea conveniente. Esta ayuda puede ser económica, moral, espiritual, o material.[15]

In accordance with these stated objectives, the rules for membership stated that persons applying for membership were required to be males, seventeen years or older, and of Spanish American descent, at least on one side of their family.[16] Furthermore, they had to be devout Catholics, interested in working for the good of society, and responsible for their own actions.

In light of these religious, physical and cultural qualifications, the stated objectives of improving the moral fiber of the community, providing wholesome recreation, caring for the unfortunate and battling communism, the Club Artístico Guadalupano appears to have been more of a lay religious order or brotherhood rather than what one would ordinarily expect a community theater group to be. The plays chosen to be produced by the group were selected under the criteria concordant with these principles.[17] Thus, Jacinto Benevente's *El Nietecito* was seen to be morally uplifting, while Alfonso Sastre's *El Pan de Todos* was attractive because it attacked communism. Of course, the club's grandest endeavors were the Our Lady of Guadalupe plays that became rituals every December. Another aspect of the social, moral, and religious commitment made by the club was the improvisation of *sainetes* and comical sketches that touched on community themes such as the air pollution problem and local politics. Religious guidance and assistance was provided by Father Miguel Ortiz at first and later by Father Peter R. Meade.[18]

While various dramatic improvisations by the Club Artístico Guadalupano were presented on an informal basis, the formal productions for the community at large have been documented in the pages of the *Latin Times* as follows: five performances of *El Milagro del Tepeyac* with a *sainete cómico* entitled *Mañana te lo devuelvo*, 1960-1962; a number of performances of Jacinto Benevente's *El nietecito* along with a *sainete* entitled *Robo a la Alta Escuela*, 1961; and two performances of *Las rosas del Tepeyac*, 1967-1968. In addition, three plays were in rehearsal for an extended period of time but were never produced in public: *El pan de todos, La barca sin pescador* and *Yo la maté*. The club's library was also in possession of a number of other plays that the group had intended to perform,[19] most of which were either ordered by mail from Librería Porrúa in Mexico City or from an uncle of one of the club members who was a professional actor in Mexico. The text of *El nietecito*, however, was obtained from the East Chicago Public Library.

The admission price of $.75 to $1.00 for a typical Club Artístico Guadalupano function entitled a spectator to more than just a
dramatic performance; it also included a varied program of poetry,
folk dancing, songs and speeches. The program at which *El nietecito* was presented included after the play's performance the following acts known as the "Fin de Fiesta":

I.  *El nietecito*—Obra dramática en dos actos de Don Jacinto
    Benavente.
II.  Jarabe Tapatío . . . por la senorita Mercedes Sánchez y
    Víctor Manuel Martínez.
III.  "Los motivos del lobo" . . . declamación por el Sr. Ro-
    dolfo Camacho.
IV.  Número musical a cargo del Sr. Angel Muñoz.
V.  *Robo a la alta escuela* . . . sainete cómico en un acto.
VI.  Presentación de los Hermanitos Cantú.
VII.  "Reír Llorando" . . . declamación interpretada por el Sr.
    Víctor Manuel Martínez.
VIII.  "Torna Sorrento" . . . canción interpretada por el Sr. Ro-
    berto Padilla.
IX.  Todo el grupo participante en este evento hará acto de pre-
    sencia en el escenario para despedir a la concurrencia.[20]

But the club's activities were by no means limited to producing
plays. The members and their talents were cultural resources that
the community would tap for the celebration of various religious
and cultural events. The participation by club members in these
events took the form of oratory, singing the Mexican National An-
them, the recitation of poetry, the running of bazaars and ker-
messes, etc. Moreover, it seems that club members, especially the
president, Víctor Manuel Martínez, were looked upon as experts in
"culture" in general, but especially Mexican national culture. The
members were continuously sought after to preside at important
community affairs and thus the club's constitution set rigid guide-
lines for the public comportment of its members. In all respects
they were to serve as models for the Mexican community.

Unfortunately, the Club Artístico Guadalupano met its final
demise through lack of interest, approximately ten years after its

inception. Signs of growing disintegration had always been present, even as early as 1961 when the president and principal founder, Víctor Manuel Martínez, tendered his resignation in protest of the lack of commitment by his fellow members. In his letter of resignation he refers to the ideals behind the club's founding and his growing disillusionment with the lack of responsibility to those ideals:

> Desde poco tiempo después de mi llegada a este país y viendo como nuestra colectividad hispanoamericana ocupaba un lugar inferior entre las clases sociales con las que nos toca convivir, un pensamiento de idealista si ustedes quieren, comenzó a tomar vida en mi mente, y ese sueño que consiste en poder llegar algún día a formar una organización fuertemente unida y dedicada en todo momento a trabajar por la elevación de los niveles *espirituales, morales*, y *culturales*, en primer término, de sus miembros para que estos sirvieran de ejemplo a la comunidad, la que, al recibir el impacto producido por la conducta y carácter firme de los socios, buscaría también la manera de alcanzar esa superación y apoyaría en todo, la doctrina de una organización constituida verdaderamente para lograr el adelanto en los niveles anteriormente enumerados. Esta fue otra idea que abrigaba mi mente cuando se iniciaba apenas la integración del Club Artístico Guadalupano. Pero desgraciadamente esa nota de acrisolada seriedad de que todo el grupo dio muestra en un principio, se ha venido desvaneciendo en forma tal, que casi nada, o mejor dicho, nada de lo planeado se ha verificado y todo se ha convertido en un simple juego infantil en el cual me es imposible seguir tomando parte y contra el, yo me declaro en completo desacuerdo, condenando dicha actitud porque convierte dicho juego, al club, de organización seria en un simple y sencillo "kindergarden."[21]

But after a hiatus of productions from 1963 through 1966, the club managed to serve the community for another two years in 1967 and 1968, after which it met its final demise. Perhaps the unusual longevity of the club, in comparison with efforts by other groups, was due to the rigid discipline that was built into the organization by the constitution, the continued renewal of loyalty through such acts as repetition of the membership oath, and a vision of their activities as part of a religious and moral mission, besides a cultural one. The sense of mission is all-important to sustain community movements, even in a community theater. It is a strong sense of mission that also sustains today's Chicano theater throughout the United States.

During the 1950's, a new Spanish-speaking population, the Puerto Ricans, began to appear in northwest Indiana, and by the late fifties there was already news of dramatic presentations along the lines followed previously by the Mexicans. That is, Puerto Rican community theater was also associated with the Church and mutual aid societies. Whereas the primary religious and dramatic focus of the Mexican community was the celebration of the Apparition of Our Lady of Guadalupe, for the Puerto Ricans the central religious feast was the Adoration of the Magi, celebrated annually on the sixth of January. In 1959, for example, East Chicago's Brotherhood Social Club was featuring *Los Tres Reyes Magos*, performed by its youth committee with assistance from Vicente Valjaló, the Chilean who was also participating with the Teatro Experimental Talía and the Club Artístico Guadalupano.[22] Another example of these early presentations was a more formalized organization, Grupo Artístico Ciro Ríos, that performed *El nacimiento de N.S. Jesucristo* at the American Legion Post in East Chicago in 1960.[23]

But by far the most serious dramatic activity in the Puerto Rican community of northwest Indiana was to be found at the Primera Iglesia Cristiana. When the Puerto Rican baptists started migrating to the area in the 1940's, they attended the Segunda Iglesia Bautista of East Chicago where they participated in Christmas dramatizations with the Mexican baptists. Later on, however, the Puerto Ricans founded their own Church, the Primera Iglesia Cristiana, with a branch in Gary and one in East Chicago. The Gary church soon became a center of religious theater. Although the Mexican Baptist Church in East Chicago had traditionally produced Christmas plays and pageants based on scripts written by Latin American authors, obtained through the Baptist Publishing House in El Paso, Texas, the Christmas dramatizations at the Primera

Iglesia Cristiana soon lay a foundation for more sophisticated and formalized drama.[24]

During the period from 1956 through 1965, the Primera Iglesia Cristiana of Gary served as the monthly meeting place for the youth fellowship movement of the Gary, East Chicago and Chicago branches of the church.[25] The "Juventud en Marcha" would draw gatherings of three hundred people who, after study sessions, would hold choir practice and informal socials. A group of youths soon began presenting skits on various religious and secular themes to the gathering. The church-related subjects that were dramatized included "the end of the world," the ills of money and materialism, and Judgment Day. However, such subjects as politics and upcoming elections were also developed dramatically by the group.

This initial interest soon led to the group writing and producing its own plays. Rubén Cruz, from the Chicago church, wrote a two-act play entitled *Creo*, which, set in a New York barrio, was the story of a delinquent Puerto Rican youth's reformation after discovering Christ. The play had three performances in 1964 and was followed by two performances of a play entitled *Trapped*, written and directed by Carmelo Meléndez. *Trapped* was the story of a young Puerto Rican experiencing the generation gap and a cultural identity crisis at home and in church. A third member of the group to take an important role in assisting with the directing was the Gary minister's son, Luis Ferrer. He, as well as Cruz and Meléndez, had considerable experience performing in and directing Christmas plays. Their dramatic avocation was quite successful while it lasted, drawing audiences of three hundred people, even when performing at public schools and community centers. But the activities ended when differences arose between the Gary and East Chicago denominations and thus curtailed inter-church cooperation with the youth fellowship movement.

Today Luis Ferrer is the minister of the Gary Primera Iglesia Cristiana where he still directs and writes Christmas plays.[26] Rubén Cruz is now the minister of the Chicago Primera Iglesia Cristiana, as well as producer and host of "Oiga Amigo," a WLS-TV weekly television program. Carmelo Meléndez is today a civil rights leader and a principal member of a Gary-East Chicago Chicano and Puerto Rican theater group, El Teatro Desengaño del Pueblo.

71

Today, the Christmas dramatizations continue, although sporadically, in Gary and East Chicago. Mother's Day is celebrated at the Union Benéfica Mexicana with an occasional dramatization of "El brindis del Bohemio." But the 1970's have brought a new type of drama to northwest Indiana, one that embodies a religious dedication similar to that of earlier endeavors, but more oriented to politics and the Latino civil rights struggle. Since 1971, El Teatro del Barrio, a Chicano theater group from South Chicago, has been performing in the area. On occasion, groups from the Southwest like El Teatro de Artes Chicanos from San Antonio, have also toured Indiana. But most noteworthy of all is the existence since 1972 of the Teatro Desengaño del Pueblo, a Chicano and Puerto Rican theater group that has patterned itself after Chicano theaters in the Southwest. The director and founder of the theater group, Nicolás Kanellos, was previously a member of the Teatro Chicano de Austin before moving to Indiana. The other members are from the Gary and East Chicago communities. One of the leading members, Carmelo Meléndez, had considerable previous experience in other types of community theater. Some of the other actors were members of the mutual aid societies and churches that sponsored the earlier productions. The Teatro Desengaño del Pueblo is the latest phase of unbroken tradition of community theater, even to the extent that one of its actresses is the daughter of a former actress of the Cuadro Dramático del Círculo de Obreros Católicos "San José" before the depression.

This brief examination of the last fifty years of Latino community theater in northwest Indiana makes possible various conclusions regarding the role of theater in urban, Spanish-speaking communities. First of all, dramatic productions are seen as important to the community and therefore are most often sponsored or identified with the two central institutions of the Latino community: the church and the mutual aid society. As has been so often corroborated in the past, the productions go beyond mere recreation to serve as forums or examples of certain moral, religious and cultural principles that the community holds dear. In its latest phase, this didactic and moralistic mission has become more politically and socially oriented through theater groups modeled after

Chicano theaters of the Southwest. Finally, the unbroken tradition of community theater has provided an outlet in the community for the immense creativity of its citizens who, no longer just producing plays by Spanish, French and Latin American authors, have also written their own plays and used drama to mold public opinion on important community issues. At every stage, the development of the theatrical avocation in the community has been indicative of the community's growth and transformation from Mexican "colonia" to Chicano and Puerto Rican barrio.

[1]Considerable information about these groups is contained in the pages of *El Amigo del Hogar*, a weekly newspaper published in Indiana Harbor from 1925 to 1930.

[2]On March 20, 1927, *El Amigo del Hogar* announced the *zarzuela*, *El Puñao de rosas* by an unnamed touring company; on April 1, 1928, the *cuadro de variedades*, "Cuanhtemoc" on tour from Chicago; on October 7, 1928, Alfaro Sigueiros, an expert in "tsicofonomímica." This is just a brief sampling of the varied spectacles that were constantly presented to the community by touring showmen and theatrical companies.

[3]*Estatutos del Círculo de Obreros Católicos "San José",* (Indiana Harbor, 1925), p. 16.

[4]*El nido ajeno*, by Jacinto Benavente, and *El que nace para ochavo* (March 13, 1927); *Hernán o la vuelta del cruzado*, by Fernando Calderón (April 2, 1927); *El Conde de Monte-Cristo*, by Alexandre Dumas (April 30, 1927); *El caudal de los hijos; La Mujer X*, by Bisson (November 19, 1927); *El juez de su sangre*, by Eduardo Vidal y Valencia and José Roca y Roca (February 19, 1928); *Los pobres de Madrid*, Manual Ortiz de Pinedo (February 24, 1928); and *Santa Inés*, a Silesian play (May, 1928).

[5]Mrs. Consuelo C. de Figueroa, who acted in many of the Cuadro Dramático's productions, provided me with information on this.

[6]See: Enrique de Olivarría y Ferrari, "Nómina de los teatros capitalinos y de las obras o espectáculos en ellos ofrecidos desde octubre de 1911 hasta el 30 de junio de 1961," *Reseña Historica del Teatro en Mexico*, Vol. V (México: Editorial Porrúa, 1961), pp. 3381-3680.

[7]Mrs. Irene González, a former participant in community productions, has informed me in an interview that a certain Professor Alonso, who gained his livelihood by teaching Spanish to first generation Mexican children at the Sociedad Benito Juárez, also wrote and directed plays for adults on the themes of "Benito

Juárez" and "Los Niños Héroes" during the late 1930's. These were produced, yearly, usually in connection with the celebration of Mexican Independence.

[8]Although there is no documentation to confirm the existence of teather in the 1940's, Eduardo Curiel, a former actor in community productions, informed me in an interview that a certain Sr. Centeno was an active director of a theater group in Gary during the late forties.

[9]Sister Cordelia Marie was my source on this matter.

[10]*Latin Times*, 28 December 1962.

[11]Terry Serna, "Harbor Lights," *Vida Latina*, April, 1963, p. 6.

[12]According to the *Latin Times*, 28 April 1961, Gildardo Peral and Ramiro García had taken part in a dramatization of "El Brindis del Bohemio" for Mother's Day at the Unión Benéfica Mexicana.

[13]*Latin Times*, 28 April 1961.

[14]*Latin Times*, 12 May 1961.

[15]Article 2 of the Constitution of the Club Artístico Guadalupano obtained from past president, José Camacho.

[16]Article 5 of the Constitution of the Club Artístico Guadalupano.

[17]The following plays were ordered from Librería Porrúa, Mexico City, on October 29, 1961: *Cena de Navidad*, by López Rubio; *Juego de niños*, by Ruiz Iriarte; *Las maletas del más alla*, by Félix Ross; *Tánger*, by Calvo Sotelo; *En las manos del hijo*, by Pemán; *Julio César*, by Shakespeare; *La mordaza*, by Sastre; *Crimen Perfecto*, by Knott; *La dama de las camelias*, by Dumas; *Judas*, by Franco Fochi; *El silencio de Dios*, by Sastre; *Don Juan Tenorio*, by Zorrilla; and *La loca de la casa*, by Pérez Galdós.

[18]The Club Artístico Guadalupano also received minor financial assistance in the form of short-term loans from Our Lady of Guadalupe Church.

[19]Besides those ordered from Porrúa, the following titles were still in the possession of the former president, Mr. José Camacho: *La boronda*, by Javier de Burgos; *José María Pacheco*, by José María Pemán; *El pan de todos*, by Alfonso Sastre; *Luzbel*, (Anonymous); *Fabiola o los mártires de Roma*, (Anonymous); *Jusepe, El zagal o el nacimiento del Mesías*, (Anonymous); and *No me esperes mañana*, (Anonymous).

[20]Taken from a program in the files of the organization in the care of past president, Mr. José Camacho.

[21]Letters of resignation by Mr. Víctor Manuel Martínez, in the files of the Club Artístico Guadalupano.

[22]*Latin Times*, 24 December 1959.

[23]*Latin Times*, 31 December 1960.

[24]Examples of the texts obtained from the Baptist Publishing House in El Paso are these that were obtained from Reverend Luis Ferrer of the Primera Iglesia Cristiana: *Dramatizaciones cristianas (Para presentar en las festividades religiosas más importantes y en las reuniones sociales de carácter cristiano)*, México, D.F.: Casa Unida de Publicaciones, 1956; Julia Anaya Echegoyen, *Hemos visto su estrella*, Mexico, D.F.: Ediciones las Américas, s.d.; Daniel Aguilar

Ochoa, *Destellos de Navidad*, d.f.; David Orea Luna, *Noche tempestuosa. Drama de Navidad en cinco cuadros*, México, D.F.: Casa Unida de Publicaciones, 1961; William M. Lessel, *No hay lugar en el mesón. Dramita de Navidad en tres escenas*, Medellín, Colombia: Librería La Aurora, s.d.

[25]From interviews with Carmelo Meléndez and Reverend Luis Ferrer.

[26]He has directed *El nacimiento de Cristo*, taken from *Dramatizaciones cristianas, la historia de Navidad*; Dorothy Clark Wilson's *Los que moran en tinieblas*, and his own play, *Despidiendo el año viejo*.

# A Brief Overview of the Mexican-American
# Circus in the Southwest

Early circus history in the Southwest of the United States owes much to the circus as it developed in Mexico. Even today Mexicans are represented substantially in circuses around the country. The Mexican American circus experience is one that has benefited from a diverse series of roots and influences. Hernán Cortez's chronicler, Bernal Díaz del Castillo, recognized circus-type diversions at the court of Montezuma, emperor of the Aztecs. From then on the circus activities of the American Indians and those of the Spaniards were blended to give a distinct character to the circus as it developed in Mexico and later in the Southwest. On this early base of *mestizo* circus culture the nineteenth and twentieth centuries added layers of Italian, English and Anglo-American influence, until finally after World War II, the Mexican-American circus ceased to exist and the *Mexicanos* were assimilated into the large American circus companies or they left the circus life completely.

The indigenous roots of the Mexican-American circus can be identified in the entertainments by dwarfs, buffoons and a type of clown that Bernal Díaz documented as existing in Pre-Columbian Mexico. There also existed an acrobatic religious ritual that involved flyers called "voladores" descending like birds from a high revolving platform while another acrobat danced atop the tiny platform and played a flute and small drum. As the American Indian religions were supplanted by Christianity, this ritual became a secular circus act that persists to this day. The early mestizo circus was called "compañía de voladores," "compañía de volantines" or simply, "la maroma"; this last term was derived from the rope tied to the flyers.[1] Thus the acrobats also came to be known as "maromeros."

The European circus tradition begins in the New World with the Spaniards' introduction of roving minstrels, saltimbanquis, juglars, etc., during the colonization period. By 1670, *maromeros* were noted as performing at bullfights in Mexico City, and by

1769, a clown known as "el loco de los toros" had already evolved (María y Campos, 78-79). This figure is probably an early predecessor of the rodeo clown of today. By 1785, the first *compañía* de volantines was documented as having performed at a theater in Mexico City, followed by the performance of musical and dramatic pieces by the regular actors of the theatre (María y Campos, 18). This mixture of circus and theatrical spectacles was to characterize the Mexican circus from then on. In 1791 there appeared a circus made up of totally Mexican talent, the Compañía de Volantines del País. In 1792, a Compañía de Volantines featured La Romántica in a balancing act, a clown dressed as a woman who danced *jarabe*, leapers, slight of hand artists and even a shadow play (María y Campos, 20-22).

At this time and well into the nineteenth century, circuses would stage their performances at theatres and at bullrings. In 1833, Carlos E. Green's circus, originating from the northeastern United States, was the first to feature pantomimes, such as the one entitled "Don Quijote y Sancho Panza" (María y Campos, 24). Also at this time, the *payaso* or *gracioso* of the Spanish theatrical tradition was featured singing popular songs in the circus. The most famous of these *payasos*, José Soledad Aycardo, appeared in the Mexican circus in 1852 to dominate it for the next five decades. El Chole Aycardo's diverse talents included horsemanship, acrobatics, gymnastics, *maroma*, acting and composing and reciting poetry on topical themes. In fact, his is the most important contribution to the evolution of the Mexican clown as a poet and satirist. Aycardo organized all of his circus' acts and also directed and acted in operettas, *pastorelas* and five-act melodramas. Aycardo combined European-type circus with *maroma* and theatre.

During the second half of the nineteenth century, the Mexican circus received important influences from Italian, English and Anglo-American circuses that performed in Mexico. Most noteworthy of all was the introduction of the English-type clown by the Chiarini Circus in 1867 (María y Campos, 150). The clown wore baggy pants, a face made up with flour and a red wig with three lumps of curls on the forehead. Chiarini was also important for having integrated Mexican acts into the show. In 1869 he introduced the Bell Family from England (María Campos, 165). Five-year-old Ricardo Bell was to become the most famous clown in Mexican history and was to become the patriarch of a large and very famous circus family. Although Ricardo Bell was born in England, he grew up in Mexico, he and his children intermarried with Mexicans, and for all intents and purposes he and his family became Mexican. In 1873 Chiarini also introduced the Orrin Family which originated in England and the northeastern United States (María y Campos, 168). The Orrins also founded a circus dynasty in Mexico. The Orrins' popularity virtually drove the more traditional Mexican circuses from the capital. Only when it was on tour did such companies as Ortiz (later to reappear in the United States Southwest), directed by Jesús Ortiz, perform in Mexico City. At this time the Rivas Brothers were also appearing with Chiarini and Bell; after the turn of the century they would tour their own circus in the United States Southwest.

In the nineteenth century there existed a more humble, poor man's circus that traveled the poorer neighborhoods of Mexico City and the interior and set up a small tent or *carpa* to house its performances. The term *carpa* is ancient Quechua for an awning made of interwoven branches.[2] In Spanish it signifies canvas cover, tent, and finally, a type of folksy and down-to-earth circus. During the Mexican Revolution, actors and clowns from the more established theatres and circuses took refuge in the *carpas* where the pantomimes originated by Ricardo Bell and the satire of Aycardo fermented to bring about the creation of the satirical, often political, review which starred the character that today is recognized as the Mexican national clown: the *pelado* or naked one, penniless, underdog. Somewhat reminiscent of Charlie Chaplin and best exemplified by Cantinflas, the *peladito* improvises a dialog which "brings to the scene the fine humor of the people, their critical spirit, their complaints and desires; and the people, in turn, upon seeing their own existence portrayed on the stage, cooperate directly with the comics, conversing with them, proposing problems for their inventive spirits to solve, rewarding and punishing them, with crude sincerity."[3] The themes of these improvised comic routines were the high cost of living, political scandals, the treachery of political leaders, etc. ". . . the true voice of the people is heard in the *carpas*, and what no newspaper dare print is said with open

Beatriz "La Chata" Noloesca and Pedro "Ramirín" González González.

Don Fito, the *peladito* of the Carpa García.

Carpa García chorus girls.

frankness by these traveling comics."[4] The *carpas* thus functioned as popular tribunals.

From the 1850s on there is considerable documentation of touring *compañías de volantines* and *maromas* throughout the Southwest. The earliest note comes from Monterey, California, in 1846, concerning *maromas*.[5] Gipson mentions a Mexican circus of acrobats, clowns, rope walkers and stock characters of devils and skeletons in Tucson form 1853 to 1854, and attests that by the 1870s the Mexican circus was the most popular and frequent type of entertainment in Tucson.[6] In California during the 1850s a Circo de Los Angeles appears with the Spanish clown Nicolás Martínez.[7] Also both Chiarini and Orrin made their way to San Francisco in the 1860s, where they were already performing with Hispanic acts. The Real Circo Italiano de Chiarini in 1868 included the following acts: Belén and Teodoro Cuba (the Cubas were called Ethiopians, but they were probably black Cubans), Teófilo Dominguez riding Indio Comanche, the equestrian dwarf Vicente Torres, equestrians Señoritas Ruiz and Martínez, and M.M. Silvestre climbing the spiral mountain (volantín?).[7]

The earliest reference to the Mexican circus in Texas is the following comment from the San Antonio *Ledger*, November 8, 1852: "The Mexican circus is with us. We knew in our hearts the season for fun and jolity was about to commence." The comment seems to indicate that the San Antonio public was familiar with the Mexican circus and we can probably assume that these circuses had performed in San Antonio prior to this date. Years later, the Mexican circus seems to have lost some of its appeal; *The Daily Herald*, December 31, 1869, published this reaction to the Great American Havanna Circus Company: "For once—the *Herald* and the *Express* agree on the merits of the Mexican circus—that it is humbug." From this time until the 1950s, San Antonio seems to have been an important show town for Mexican circuses as well as a home base for some of them.

During the period of the Mexican Revolution, many circuses began touring north of the border and chose places like San Antonio and Los Angeles for their home bases. After the hostilities ceased, some returned to Mexico, but others remained in the United States where they had established lucrative circuits. A fruitful avenue for many Mexican circus performers was the Mexican vaudeville circuit in the United States. Some of the performers even made their way into the American and Canadian vaudeville circuits during the 1920s and '30s. The Bell family, after relocating in the Southwest, for instance, not only toured the vaudeville circuits but also bought a theatre in Los Angeles to house its own performances and those of other touring companies. Even the great Escalante Circus at times booked some of its family members into vaudeville houses to raise some extra funds. Other circuses that moved north were the Ortiz Brothers and the Rivas Brothers. Of all of them, the Escalante Circus seems to have had the greatest popularity and longevity in the Southwest, performing from the 1900s well up into the 1950s.

But the type of Mexican circus that survived the longest in the United States was the small, family-based *carpa* that performed along the Mexican-American border. For the most part the *carpas* survived the Depression, Repatriation and the other ecomonic and social forces that put Mexican and Hispanic entertainments out of business during the 1930s and 1940s. Some *carpas* continued to perform along the border into the 1960s and even followed the migrant labor stream north. Today there is still an occasional *carpa* that visits the towns of the Rio Grande Valley.

Probably because of their small size, bare-bones style and or-ganization around a family unit, the *carpas* could manage themsel-ves better than the larger circuses. Furthermore, they were able to cultivate smaller audiences in the most remote areas. The *carpas* became in the Southwest an important Mexican-American, popular culture institution. Their comic routines became a sounding board for the culture conflict that Mexican Americans felt in language usage, assimilation to American tastes and life-styles, discrimina-tion in the United States and *pocho*-status in Mexico. Out of these types of conflicts in the popular entertainments arose the stereotype of the Pachuco, a typically Mexican-American figure. The *carpa* also preserved the format of the Mexican vaudeville review (*revista*) that in the late sixties would find new life in Chicago theatre. El Teatro Campesino, for instance, not only resuscited the *carpa* in *La gran carpa de la familia Rascuachi* but also built its action around a *peladito*, Jesús Pelado. In fact, San Antonio's 1979 Chicano theatre festival was dedicated to La Carpa García and some of the local circus' comic routines were revived. Finally, the *carpas* were a refuge for theatrical and circus people of all types. These artists could ride out the Depression, Repatriation and World War II with a steady although meager employment, doing something akin to their regular acts. More importantly, these cultural arts were preserved by the *carpas* for the post-War generation that was to forge a new relationship to the larger American culture. The Carpa García retired its tents around 1948.

The following is a preliminary inventory of Mexican circuses performing primarily around California and Texas prior to World War II:

*Gran Circo Escalante Hermanos.* Founded some time around 1917 and lasting well into the 1950s, with Los Angeles as its base, the Escalante circus was probably the most widely known of the Mexican circuses, performing throughout the Southwest in its own tents. The Escalantes were originally acrobats, but their tents housed a great variety of acts, including dramatic pieces. Among the featured groups was El Troupe Piña in 1920, formerly with Orrin. The circus' impresario was Mariano Escalante (1881-1961) and its clowns were Cara Sucia, Tony and Chamaco. In 1934, probably affected by the Depression and Repatriation, the company announced that it was going to Mexico (*La Opinión*, Los Angeles, August 10, 1934). It later returned to the United States and in 1950 *Billboard* brought down the final curtain for Yolanda Escalante (b. 1928) and in 1961 for Mariano.

*Los Hermanos Bell.* During the Mexican Revolution the Bell family moved to the United States where for many years it toured the vaudeville circuits adapting its music, dance, pantomime and dramatic talents, its feats of strength, magic and other spectacles to the stage. Among the sketches that were salvaged from the circus show were "El Espejo Roto" (The Broken Mirror), "La Princesa del Hawaii" (The Hawaiian Princess), "Gabinete Dental" (The Dentist's Office) and "Barbería filharmónica" (an original of the late Ricardo Bell, Sr.) and many others.

A typical program was (such as would be performed at the Teatro Novel in 1920): Nelly Bell (dancer), Jorge Bell (ventriloquist), Ricardo Bell, Jr. (violinist), Oscar Bell (impressionist, espe-

# Circo Escalante Hnos.

## COMPAÑIA DE BAILE Y VARIEDADES

Carpas Situadas en el extremo oeste de la calle Congress

## Hoy-Martes 29 de Marzo-Hoy

Regia Funcion de Gracia --- Notable Acontecimiento

### LO MEJOR DE LO MEJOR

## Funcion de Beneficio

Predomina la Nobleza, Predomina el Humanitarismo

### ¡Ojo!    ¡Ojo!    ¡Ojo!

### AL PUBLICO

Habiendo acordado el comité "Grijalva" el que encargado está para colectar fondos de la hospitalaria colonia mexicana, con objeto de llevar hasta el fin la defensa judicial de un hermano de raza, ha ocurrido, repito, a la compañía Escalante Hnos., solicitando encarecidamente, de dicha empresa, una funcion de gracia, funcion de beneficio, para fortalecer más los fondos destinados a tan noble y humanitaria acción, los hermanos Escalante, sin poner objeción alguna, gustosos y satisfechos de tan digno proceder, han accedido orgullosos de poder contribuir con su pequeño grano de arena y al mismo tiempo cumplir con un deber sagrado.

Esperamos del amable y benévolo público que nos favorece, ocurran a esta simpatica velada que tiene por objeto tan noble y magnanimo principio; no dudando que el público tucsonense siempre se ha distinguido por su caritativo proceder, y por lo mismo, recordamos no olvidar que tan enorme pena puede acabar la vida de una amable esposa y amabilisimos hijos que deja tras sí a sufrir inexplicables peripecias. Anticipamos las más debidas gracias a todo aquel que pudiera prestar una mano ayudadora a quien tanto lo necesita.

ESCALANTE HNOS.                    COMITE "GRIJALVA."

ALFREDO GRIJALVA

Trapecios -- Barras -- Alambristas -- Bailes -- Cantos Couplet, Zarzuela, Recitaciones, Excentricos y Pantomimas esta Noche.

No Faltando los Siempre Graciosos y Ocurrentes "Cara Sucia," "Tony" y "Chamaco."

Al Circo esta Noche a Contribuir con tan Noble Cometido

### PRECIOS DE ENTRADA

| | |
|---|---|
| Entrada General | 50c |
| Niños | 25c |
| Asientos Reservados -- Ex. | 25c |

**Poster, Circo Escalante.**

cially of Charlie Chaplin); all of the nine Bells acted, sang and played diverse musical instruments together.

In 1925 when they played San Antonio's Teatro Nacional, they also featured clown acts. In 1927 Ricardo Bell, Jr., bought the Teatro Capitol in Los Angeles where the family performed and also hired such acts as their long-time associates, the Areu Brothers (dancers) and Beatriz Noloesca (San Antonio-native, internationally renowned singer, dancer, actress). In fact, the Bells had at one time formed a partnership with the Areus and toured as the Compañía de Novedades Modernas Bell-Areu, which also included the famous magician Justiniani. The importance of the Bells was that they passed on many of their father's routines to Mexican-American popular culture. They continued to tour into the 1930s.

*Esqueda Brothers Show.* Active in California and Arizona throughout the 1920s, the Esqueda Show was basically an acrobatic, equestrian and vaudeville company that included the clowns Pipo, Paquito and Toni. In 1929, under impresario Juan Esqueda, the Circo Esqueda suffered a terrible accident in Nogales in which their tent's centerpole fell and injured various specators (*La Prensa*, San Antonio, August 24, 1929).

*Circo Rivas Brothers.* Probably from interior Mexico and associated there with Chiarini, the Rivas Brothers are documented as having performed in the Southwest under impresario L.P. Rivas, at least from 1917 to 1921. Their acts included the clown El Segundo Robledillo (Manuel Macias), the clown Ferrin (Amador Fierro), María Rivas on the trapeze, and various poney, monkey, vaudeville and pantomime routines.

*P. Pérez Show Circo y Variedades.* Documented as having performed in Los Angeles in 1923, the circus included the Pérez sisters with song and dance, and clowns Cristobalito, Rivanito and Tamborini.

*Circo Azteca de los Hermanos Olvera.* The only documentation that has been uncovered regarding this show is a note of its performances from 1918 to 1922 in Los Angeles, Agua Prieta and Douglas.

*Circo Carnival "Iris Show".* Documented as having appeared in Los Angeles in 1923, the Iris Show included the following: María Refugio Fuentes, song and dance; Santos Fuentes (a young girl), flyer and contortionist; Abundio Fuentes, "fuerte de altura", Daniel Rodríguez, magician; Elíseo Carrillo, "mandibulista"; and Juan Soto, actor, singer, director, impresario.

*Teatro Carpa Hermanos Rosete Aranda.* Documented as having appeared in Los Angeles in 1925, its impresarios were Carlos V. Espinel e Hijos.

*La Compañía Hermanos Ortiz.* Active from the 1920s to the late 1930s in Texas and New Mexico, in its May, 1936 performance in San Antonio it featured 12 acts, including magic and the clowns Tamborin and Rubiné. Its impresario was Emiliano Ortiz.

*Teatro Carpa Independencia, also known as Carpa Guzmán.* The Guzmán is one of the companies that used San Antonio as its home base. Its activity has been partially documented for the years 1917 and 1918. San Antonio's *La Prensa*, April 29, 1918, identifies some of the troupe members who were long time San Antonio residents: María del Carmen Guzmani, María P. de Sampers, Amelia Solsona, Manuel Sampers, Aurelio Díaz. The August 18, 1917 show featured A. Guzmani transforming himself into five different characters in an act called "Castillos en el aire," Sr. Flores on the high bar, the gymnast Mr. Sales, the comic duet Carmencita y Tiburcio, the Hermanos Olvera Guatemalan marimba quartet, singer Carmen G. de Guzmani, and a pantomime entitled "Un baile de carnaval."

*Compañía de Vaudeville Mantecón, also known as Circo Mantecón.* Documented as performing in San Antonio, Floresville, Beeville, Corpus Christi and Del Rio in 1921, their San Antonio vaudeville performance was at the Teatro Nacional on the same bill with the magician Justiniani. Also a family-based circus, the Mantecon company included twenty-eight members, many of whom belonged to the immediate family. In Del Rio, July 1921, it donated 50% of the gross for the construction of a Mexican school.

*Cuban Show (also known as Carpa Cubana, Circo Cubano).* Based in San Antonio, but also traveling as far west as California, the Cuban show existed in the 1920s and 1930s under the directorship of Virgilio Abreu. The circus included trapeze artists, rope walkers, jugglers, clowns, dancers and its own ten-piece band. According to San Antonio's *La Prensa*, July 16, 1921, the circus was advertising pantomimes on Mexican national themes for its Kingsville and Lyford, Texas performances. The various Abreu brothers—José, Virgilio, Cloe and Domingo—had broad experience during the teens with such circuses as Barnum and Bailey, Ringling Brothers, Robinson and Sells-Floto.

*Carpa García.* The best known of the San Antonio-based Mexican circuses, the Carpa García was founded in 1914 by Manuel V. García, a native of Saltillo, Mexico. It originally was called the Carpa Progresista, later the Argentina Show. Manuel, an orphan who joined the circus at age fifteen, became a trapeze artist, dancer and everything else that it took to run a small circus. Featured in the show was the famed Charro on the tight rope act. One of the comic actors of the Carpa, Pedro González ("Ramirín") later had a successful career in Hollywood westerns. The Carpa also featured the comic hoboes Don Suave and Don Fito, as well as a Pachuco type called Don Slica (slick).

*Miscellaneous shows.* Other tent shows that have been briefly documented in Texas newspapers were the Texas Show, serving the ranches around Los Ebanos, 1929; the Circo Hidalguense, noted as performing in Charlotte, Texas, in 1921; the Carpa Metropolitana in San Antonio in 1919; the Maroma Pájaro Azul, 1920s to 1930s, around Del Rio; and the Carpa Modelo, mentioned by Consuelo García of the Carpa García in an interview.[8]

[1]Armando María y Campos, *Los Payasos, poetas del pueblo* (Mexico: Ediciones Botas, 1939), p. 11.

[2]"La Carpa: El teatro popular de Mexico," *Norte: Revista Continental* (May, 1945), p. 22.

[3]"La Carpa. . . ." (my translation).

[4]*Ibid.*

[5]John Steven McGroaty, *Los Angeles from the Mountains to the Sea*, Vol. I (Chicago and New York: The American Historical Society, 1921), p.79.

[6]See Rosemary Gipson, "The Mexican Performers: Pioneer Theatre Artists in Tucson," *Journal of Arizona History*, 13/4 (Winter, 1972), pp. 235-252.

[7]*El Clamor Público*, February 6, 1858.

[8]See "La Carpa García," *Caracol* (July, 1978), pp. 5-7.

# The Origins and Development
# of Hispanic Theater in the Southwest

Until the early seventies, studies of Hispanic theater in the Southwest concentrated almost exclusively on folk drama,[1] with the bulk of published research relating to the Mexican shepherd plays or *pastorelas*.[2] It was unusual for a scholar to turn to exploring the development of professional Spanish-language theater in Southwestern history, for it was simply assumed that such a theater did not exist. Today there is still a singular absence of the Hispanic background and contribution in books on the history of the American stage and particularly in those on the origins of theater in the American West.[3] No one mentions, for example, the theater houses that bore Spanish names and that were already functioning when the first minstrels arrived from the East. Neither do they make note of the professional and amateur Spanish-language companies that represented the only available theatrical entertainment for Mexicans and Anglos alike. Moreover, histories do not discuss such events as the joining together of Hispanic and Anglo theatrical artists to offer homage to a great Mexican actor in San Francisco.

Prior to the 1970's,[4] no studies had suggested the existence of a professional, Spanish language stage in the Southwest. They overlooked the large numbers of Hispanic artists that were drawn to Hollywood and participated in both the American and the Hispanic silent film industries, as well as the success of Latin music and dance in American vaudeville, and, in addition, the large-scale commercial success of the Spanish-language stage, not only for Hispanic, but also for American theatrical entrepreneurs.

The appearance in 1965 of a farmworkers' theater, El Teatro Campesino, finally attracted attention, despite the fact that the Campesino's style of labor theater was down-to-earth, improvised and far from the lights and glamor of Broadway. Many of the Chicano players that emerged to follow Luis Valdez and El Teatro Campesino acknowledged[5] a deep-rooted tradition in the Southwest. And El Teatro Campesino took the lead, not only in reviving the neighborhood parishes' Guadalupe plays,[6] but also in fashioning its performance style after the Mexican tent theaters. These traveling circus theaters were commonly known as *carpas* or *maromas*. El Teatro Campesino developed one-act plays modeled on the *revistas* or revues that were performed in these *carpas* and also incorporated into their works the beloved, comic character of the tradition: that *pelado*.[7]

Due in great part to the success of El Teatro Campesino, scholarly interest in the history of Hispanic theater in the United States has begun to develop.[8] A handfull of serious studies now exist, although some of them have been too quick to draw conclusions from insufficient data. In an article supported only by the documentary evidence of promptbooks donated to the Benson Collection of the University of Texas and on interviews with the donor-descendants of the Hernández-Villalongín theatrical family, Brokaw states that a professional, Mexican-American stage existed principally in Texas where prior to 1910 "perhaps as many as twenty-five" troupes were found regularly and, during the Mexican Revolution years of 1910 to 1920 more Mexican troupes relocated to Texas, but most of these were short-lived.[9] He further explains that these troupes made San Antonio their center, because "overland travel in New Mexico and Arizona was very hazardous at that time because of the active hostility of Commanche, Apache, and Kiowa Indians," and also that "one imagines that during the nineteenth century there was less *teatro* activity there (California) than in Texas because of the relative distance of the two states from Mexico."[10] Furthermore, even while emphasizing that sufficient research has not yet been conducted, he nevertheless proffers the following chronology for the history of Mexican American theater:

> . . . 1848 to 1890, which saw the decline of the vestigial Spanish theater that had remained after independence; 1890 to 1918, which saw the birth of a distinctly Mexican theater; and 1918 to the present, which saw the decline of the Mexican tradition and its replacement by a Mexican American theater.[11]

Brokaw concludes that the theater received its death-blow in the 1920's "almost as if a switch had been turned off"[12] due to "the economic dislocations of the First World War. The availability of

Mexican films, and some degree of cultural assimilation on the part of Mexican Americans led to the decline and fall of the professional Hispanic theater. . . ."[13] And further, "The *teatros* ceased and theatrical production in the Spanish language was left in the hands of the church and its annual production of (sic.) *Los pastoreles.*"[14] Thus we have come full circle to considering Hispanic theater in the Southwest in relation to the religious, folk theater.

Without writing the whole history of Hispanic theater in the Southwest within this reduced format, a few of the more important moments in its development will be highlighted, with particular attention paid to documenting its origins in California, as opposed to Texas, during the 1850's and its flourishing in the Southwest, rather than its demise, during the 1920's. The following shall be posited in this study: (1) California was the most important arena for the theater's development during the nineteenth century when an Hispano-Mexican professional stage survived Anglo-American immigration and take-over and this surviving theatrical tradition served as a foundation for the Mexican immigrant theater of the first three decades of the twentieth century; (2) during these decades Los Angeles became a center where Mexican (immigrant) playwrights began to develop themes which directly related to nineteenth and twentieth century life of the Mexican/Mexican-American community in California and thus may represent today a basis for a truly Mexican-American stage.

I. Origins of the Hispanic Professional Theater in the Southwest.

We must look to California, not Texas, as Brokaw suggests, for the origins of the Hispanic professional stage in the Southwest. San Francisco and Los Angeles were more accessible to Mexico than San Antonio, for example, because of the regularity of steamship travel up and down the Pacific Coast. There is evidence that plays were being performed there as early as 1789,[15] and that at least a semi-professional theater existed by the 1840's.[16] In *The Californian's* review, October 6, 1847, of the production of *Morayma*, the newspaper mentions that "we have in Monterey, by private subscription, been again regaled with several theatrical performances," thus proving that this was not an isolated performance but, rather, one of a series.[17] The article goes on to state that officers of both the Army and Navy were in attendance. This, added to the fact that the performance was reviewed by an English-language newspaper, also confirms our belief that these entertainments were also viewed by Anglo-American residents.[18]

By the 1860's the professional stage had become so established and important to the Spanish-speaking community that companies that once toured the Mexican Republic and abroad began to settle down to serve as repertory companies in California. Such was the case of La Compañía Española de la Familia Estrella which later came under the directorship of its leading man, the great Mexican actor, Gerardo López del Castillo. The company was typical of those that toured Mexico in that it was composed of Mexican and Spanish players, staged Spanish melodrama and occasionally a Mexican or a Cuban play, and held most of its performances on Sunday evenings. The program was a complete evening's entertainment that included a three or four-act drama, song and dance, and a one-act farce or comic dialog to close the performance. The full-length plays that were the heart of the program were mostly melodramas by peninsular Spanish authors like Zorrilla, Larra and Bretón de los Herreros and, for the most part, represent texts which were readily available then and now. A few others, like *El terremoto de la Martinica*, are unknown.[19]

The leading man, and later director, was Gerardo López del Castillo, a native of Mexico City and professional actor from age fifteen. He is known as the first Mexican actor to take companies on tour outside of Mexico,[20] and by the time he had arrived in California, was already well-known throughout Mexico, the Caribbean, and Central and South America.[21] An intensely patriotic individual, López del Castillo used theatrical performances to raise funds for Zaragoza's and Juárez' liberation forces, and interrupted his theatrical career on various occasions to serve Mexico as a soldier.[22] He is also regarded as a great motivator and protector of a national dramatic art for Mexico.[23] By 1849 he was so well thought of that he was chosen to inaugurate the new theater, El Pabellón Mexicano, with a production of *El Paje*, by García Gutiérrez.[24]

In June, 1859, we find López del Castillo in Hermosillo asso-

Los Angeles' California Theatre today.

Adalberto Elías González.                    Gabriel Navarro.

ciated with the Estrella Family company and married to the daughter, Amelia, of Donato Estrella, the director of the company.[25] Donato also served as the comic actor and musical director of the troupe. The leading lady, María de los Angeles García, born in Murcia, Spain, became an actress in Mexico City at an early age and had performed at the Teatro Principal in 1844.[26] Other members of the troupe included Manuel Mancera, Rafael Rodríguez, Juan Samartín, and their wives, and Jacinto Dávila, a character actor.

By 1862 the Estrella company made San Francisco its home, although continuing to tour the area and at least once traveled down the coast to Mazatlán.[27] From March to May, 1862,[28] the company performed regularly on Sundays at Tucker's Music Academy, closing its season with a special performance at the Metropolitan Theater as part of a grand fund-raising event organized by López del Castillo for the wounded, widowed and orphaned in the Franco-Mexican War. Presumably after closing, the troupe toured in California, perhaps down to Los Angeles where an invitation had been extended.[29] It should be noted that throughout 1862 López del Castillo continued to participate in civic affairs in San Francisco, where he was serving as President of the Junta Patriótica Mexicana de San Francisco; thus the company could not have traveled too far and widely.[30]

Our bits and pieces of newspapers place the Estrella Family and López del Castillo on stage in San Francisco again in June, 1863, able to perform, it seems, only after the steamship Orizaba had brought the company a re-enforcement in the Mexican actor, José de Jesús Díaz.[31] The fragmented record shows performances by what is now Castillo's Compañía Española at the Teatro Americano during 1863 and 1864.[32] The last word of Castillo in California concerns his departure with his company, which still included his in-laws, on December 30, 1864, to perform in Mazatlán, with the writer of the article for El Nuevo Mundo wishing him a speedy return to his wife and home in San Francisco.

When the López del Castillo company returned to San Francisco[33], and how much longer they resided there is not certain.[34] Ten years later he surfaces again in Mexico City actively promoting the creation of a national dramatic literature. He performed in 1874 and 1875 at the head of a company in the Teatro Nuevo Mexico,[35] and later directed a company that included Amelia and Donato Estrella at the newly founded Liceo Mexicano in 1867.[36] He risked his career in 1876 to perform Alberto G. Bianchi's political play *Martirios del pueblo*,[37] the same play that had resulted in the author's imprisonment. Of the elderly Lopez del Castillo, María y Campos wrote:

> El público ovacionaba al gran cómico, comediante nacionalista, en la escena y fuera del teatro, que tuvo en su época, su público, y que murió pobre, pero sin abandonar la escena nacional, para la que vivía, ambicionando que fuera comprendida y estimada en lo que era y valía. Su gallarda actitud causaba risas, a pesar de lo bien intencionada y patriota. Aspiraba a lo más noble y justo, a un México para los mexicanos.[38]

Los Angeles, another coastal city, also developed an Hispanic theater early. Unlike what seems to have been the case in San Francisco, Los Angeles' Hispanic community owned and operated its own theatrical houses by the 1870's: The Teatro Alarcón[39] and the Teatro de la Merced. This fact by itself may indicate that Hispanic theatrical activity in Los Angeles got its start earlier than in San Francisco. One other house, Turn Verein, previously used for English-language and perhaps German productions, became a favorite Spanish-language house in the late 1870's. Although, as in San Francisco, a professional stage was functioning in Los Angeles in the 1860's,[40] the newspapers that have been preserved present a more complete picture of two companies[41] that were locally based in the late 1870's: The Compañía Dramática Española, directed first by José Pérez García and later by Pedro C. de Pellón, and the Compañía Dramática Española, directed by Angel de Mollá. Both companies competed for use of El Teatro de la Merced, with Mollá moving in 1877 to Turn Verein.

The José Pérez company was active in the Southwest during the years 1875 to 1878, including Hermosillo and Ures in Sonora, Mexico, and Tucson, Arizona, on its itinerary,[42] with Los Angeles possibly as its home base. The members of the company were: Doña Jesús de Terán, leading lady; José Pérez García, leading man and director; Pedro Castillo y Pellón, comic actor; Elena Mancera and Dolores Rodríguez, dancers. Documentation of the company's performances begins on February 27, 1876, with its performance of *Lázaro el mudo*, through the September 5, 1876, performance of *Arturo o Amor de madre*, in two acts, and *Maruja*, in one act.[43] Starting with the May 31 performance, Pedro C. de Pellón was the company's director, and the troupe began to alternate at La Merced with the Angel de Mollá company. After September, 1876, we lose track of the Pellón company in Los Angeles. In March, 1878, Pellón returned to Tucson and organized the town's first group of amateur actors, Teatro Recreo.[44] Included in the repertoire of his new company were some of the same plays that he had performed in Los Angeles.[45]

Gipson[46] has found that the Compañía Española de Angel de Mollá was a Los Angeles-based theater that traveled to Tucson by stagecoach every two or three years between 1873 and 1882. A letter[47] from the company, referred to in Los Angeles' *La Crónica* on April 14, 1883, shows that it was performing in Guaymas and that it soon would return to Los Angeles to fulfill a performance contract. Thus the company's circuit must also have included travel by stagecoach to points in Sonora, including Hermosillo, Guaymas and Mazatlán, where López del Castillo's troupe also performed. Regardless of performance, transportation by steamship from Mazatlán to Los Angeles was readily available. This then was a regular circuit that must have functioned at least since 1859, when the Estrella Family is recorded as performing in these towns.

The Mollá company performed at the Teatro de la Merced from June 11, 1876, until March 7, 1877.[48] From April 7, 1877, until January 2, 1884, the company performed at Turn Verein in Los Angeles.[49] After this date, nothing else is known of this troupe.


II. The Flourishing of Hispanic Theater, 1910 to the 1930's

By the turn of the century, major Spanish-language companies were performing all along the Mexico-United States border, following a circuit[50] that extended from Laredo to San Antonio and El Paso and through New Mexico and Arizona to Los Angeles, then up to San Francisco or down to San Diego. The advent of rail transportation and the automobile made theater more accessible to smaller population centers. Tent theaters and smaller make-shift companies performed along the Rio Grande Valley,[51] only occasionally venturing into the big cities to compete with the major drama and *zarzuela* (Spanish operetta) companies. By 1910 a few of the smaller cities, like Laredo, even supported their own repertory companies.[52] Theatrical activities expanded rapidly, even boomed when thousands of immigrants fled the Mexican Revolution and settled in the United States from the border states all the way up to the Midwest.[53] During the decades of the Revolution, many of Mexico's greatest artists and their theatrical companies were to take up temporary residence in the United States; however, some would never return to the homeland.

Mexican and Spanish companies, and an occasional Cuban, Argentine, or other Hispanic troupe, began to tour throughout the Southwest and as far North and East as New York, where there was also a lively Hispanic theatrical tradition. Some companies even made the coast-to-coast tour via the northern route: New York, Philadelphia, Cleveland, Detroit, Chicago, and points west to Los Angeles.[54] The company of the famed Mexican actress, Virginia Fábregas, was of particular importance in its frequent tours, because it not only performed the latest works from the theaters of Mexico City and Madrid, but some of its actors left the companies during United States tours to form their own troupes here.[55] Also, La Fábregas encouraged the development of local playwrights in Los Angeles by buying the rights to their works and performing them on tour. The Spanish companies of María Guerrero and Gregorio Martínez Sierra also made the coast-to-coast jaunts, assisted by New York booking agents and established theatrical circuits.[56] When vaudeville became popular in the twenties and thirties, the Mexican performers, many of whom previously starred in high drama and *zarzuela*, toured not only the Hispanic but the American vaudeville circuits and even performed actively in Canada.[57]

It should also be noted that many companies offered a variety of theatrical genres from *zarzuela* and operetta to drama, *comedia*, *revista*, and *variedades*. As the hundreds of companies throughout the Southwest adapted to changing tastes and economic conditions, the shifting of repertoires and the recruitment of new casts and musicians eventually brought about companies that could perform virtually anything, complementing a film with variety acts in the afternoon, producing a full-length drama in the evening, a *zarzuela* and a drama on Saturday and Sunday, different works each day, of course. The companies at times took names such as the Compañía de Comedias, Revistas y Variedades Peña-Mena, but this did not stop them from producing serious dramas like Brígido Caro's *Joaquín Murrieta*, even if this type of function was not covered in the name of the troupe.[58]

The two cities with the largest Mexican populations, Los Angeles and San Antonio, naturally became theatrical centers, the former also feeding off of the important film industry in Hollywood. In fact, Los Angeles became a manpower pool for Hispanic theater. Actors, directors, technicians and musicians from throughout the Southwest and even New York were drawn here looking for employment in the theater arts industry. Both Los Angeles and San Antonio[59] went through a period of intense expansion and building of new theatrical facilities in the late teens and early twenties. Los Angeles was able to support five major, Hispanic theater houses with programs that changed daily from 1918 until the early 1930's. The theaters and their peak years were Teatro Hidalgo (1918-1934), Teatro México, (1921-1933), Teatro Capital (1924-1926), Teatro Zendejas later Novel (1919-1924), and Teatro Principal (1921-1929). Four other theaters—Princess (1922-1926), California (1927-1934), California International (1930-1932) and Estela (1930-1932)—were also important, and at least thirteen others housed professional companies on a more irregular basis between 1915 and 1935.[60]

While it is true that in the Southwest, as in Mexico, Spanish drama and *zarzuela* dominated the stage up to the early twenties, the clamor for plays written by Mexican writers had increased to such an extent that by 1923 Los Angeles had become a center for Mexican playwriting probably unparalleled in the history of Hispanic communities in the United States. While continuing to consume plays by standard, peninsular authors like Benavente, Echegaray, Martínez-Sierra, Linares Rivas and the Quintero Brothers, the theaters and communities encouraged local writing by offering cash prizes in contests, lucrative contracts[61] and lavish productions. As the local writers became more well known, the popularity of their works brought record attendance into the theater houses.[62]

The period from 1922 to 1933 saw the emergence and box-office success of a group of playwrights in Los Angeles that was made up mainly of Mexican theatrical expatriates and newspaper men. At the center of the group were four playwrights whose works not only filled the theaters on Los Angeles' Main Street, but were also contracted throughout the Southwest and Mexico: Eduardo Carrillo, an actor; Adalberto Elias Gonzalez, a novelist; Esteban V. Escalante, a newspaperman and theatrical director; and Gabriel Navarro, poet, novelist, orchestra director, columnist for *La Opinion* and editor of *La Revista de Los Angeles*. Writers like Escalante were also important for popularizing the life of Mexicans in the United States on the stage in Mexico; for once they had returned to their homeland, they continued to compose works based on their experiences in California.[63] There were at least twenty other locally residing writers who saw their works produced on the professional stage,[64] not to mention the deluge of *revistas* that dealt with local and current themes that were written by and for the Mexican companies that presented a different program each day.[65]

The Los Angeles writers were serving a public that was hungry to see itself reflected on stage, an audience whose interest was peaked by plays relating to current events, politics, sensational crimes and, of course, the real-life epic of a people living under the cultural and economic domination of an English-speaking, American society on land that was once part of Mexican patrimony. Of course the *revistas* kept the social and political criticism directed at both the United States and Mexico within the lighter context of music and humor in such pieces as Antonio Guzmán Aguilera's *México para los mexicanos*[66] and *Los Angeles vacilador*;[67] Daniel Venegas' *El con-su-la-do* and *Maldito Jazz*; Brígido Caro's *México y Estados Unidos*;[68] Gabriel Navarro's *La Ciudad de irás y no volverás*;[69] Raúl Castell's *El mundo de las pelonas*[70] and *En el país del shimmy*;[71] and *Los efectos de la crisis, Regreso a mi tierra, Los repatriados, Whiskey, morfina y marihuana* and *El desterrado*, to mention just a few of the *revistas* of Don Catarino, who often played the role of the *pelado* in these works.[74]

The more serious, full-length plays addressed the situation of Mexicans in California on a broader, more epic scale, often in plays based on the history of the Mexican-Anglo struggle in California. Brígido Caro's *Joaquín Murrieta*, the tale of the California bandit during the Gold Rush days, not only achieved success on the professional stage,[73] but also was adopted by the community for political and cultural fund-raising activities.[74] Eduardo Carrillo's *El proceso de Aurelio Pompa* dealt with the unjust trial and sentencing of a Mexican immigrant and also was performed for fund raising purposes in the community.[76] Esteban V. Escalante's pieces, however, were more sentimental and usually written in a one-act format.[77] His three-act play, *Almas trágicas*, was a realistic drama based on local material. Gabriel Navarro also developed one-act pieces, but in a more satirical and humoristic vein.[78] But his full-length dramas, *Los emigrados* and *El sacrificio* again dealt with the epic of Mexicans in California, the latter play with a setting in 1846.[79]

By far the most prolific and respected of the Los Angeles playwrights was Adalberto Elías González, some of whose works were performed not only locally but throughout the Southwest and Mexico,[80] were made into movies[81] and translated into English.[82] His works that were produced in Los Angeles ran the gamut from historical drama to dime-novel sensationalism. The most famous of his plays, *Los amores de Ramona*, a stage adaptation of Helen Hunt Jackson's California novel, *Ramona, A Story*, broke all box-office records when it was seen by more than fifteen thousand people after only eight performances,[83] and soon became a regular item on many repertoires in the Southwest, having also been acquired by Virginia Fábregas[84] for performance on her tours. Two of his other plays deal with the life and culture of Mexicans in California: *Los misioneros* (formerly titled *La conquista de California*) and *Los expatriados*. Probably his second most successful work was the sensationalist *La asesino del martillo o la mujer tigresa*, based on news stories in 1922 and 1923.[85] On a more sentimental note are his *El sátiro*,[86] *Sangre yaqui o la mujer de los dos*, *La mal pagada*, *La desgracia del pobre*, *La flor del fandango* (based on a novel by Vargas Vila), *Nido de cuervos*[87] and *El enemigo de las mujeres*.

"La Chata" Noloesca

Romualdo Tirado.

The Mason Theatre.

Don Catarino.

Two other plays are related to the Mexican Revolution: *La muerte de Francisco Villa* and *El fantasma de la revolución*.

In truth it must be stated that the greater part of theatrical fare served purely entertainment and cultural purposes, while obliquely contributing to the expatriot community's solidarity within the context of the larger, English-speaking society. The majority of the plays produced represented the standard fare from the stages of Mexico City and Madrid. However, as can readily be seen from the above list of plays written and produced in Los Angeles, the playwrights and impresarios did not falter in dealing with controversial material. Many of their plays dealt with the historical and current circumstances of Mexicans in California from a nationalistic and at times political perspective, but always with seriousness and propriety.

The *revistas*, on the other hand, represented a genre that had developed in Mexico as a format for piquant political commentary,[88] and grievances were readily articulated in them, fun was poked at both United States and Mexican government, the Mexican Revolution was satirically reconsidered over and over again, and Mexican-American culture was contrasted with the "purer" Mexican version. This social and political commentary was carried out despite the fact that both audiences and performers were mostly immigrants and, thus, liable to deportation or repatriation. It must be remembered that the performance language was Spanish and in-group sentiments could easily be expressed, especially through the protection of satire and humor. Even such a sensitive theme as the repatriation could be treated in *revistas*. An announcement in *La Opinión* on July 23, 1934, promoted Don Catarino's *Los repatriados* as follows: "En esta comedia podrá usted saborear las graciosas tribulaciones de los repatriados." The only sign of hesitance on behalf of the impresarios was the delay of the opening in 1932 of Antonio Helú's play, *Los mexicanos se van*, which realistically depicted the forced repatriation of Mexicans from California.[89] This further substantiates the difference between the play and the *revista* as far as which of the two genres was more open to controversial issues.

It should also be emphasized that from the beginning of the Hispanic stage in California under the leadership of such men as

López del Castillo, the relationship of performers and theaters to the community and the nationality was close; the Hispanic stage served to re-enforce the sense of community by bringing all Spanish-speakers together in a cultural act: the preservation and the support of the language and the art of Mexicans and other Hispanics in the face of domination from a foreign culture. Theater, more than any other art form, became essential to promoting ethnic or national identity and solidifying the colony of expatriates and migrants. Thus, over and above the artistic, within the expatriate Mexican community, both professional and amateur theater took on specific social functions that were hardly ever assumed on the stages of Mexico City.

The professional theater houses became the temples of culture where the Mexican and Hispanic community as a whole could gather and, in the words of a theater critic of the times, "keep the lamp of our culture lighted,"[90] regardless of social class, religion or region of origin. A drama critic for San Antonio's *La Prensa*, in the April 26, 1916, edition underlined the social and nationalistic functions of the theater:

> Puede considerarse como una obra patriótica y de solidaridad de raza, el concurrir a las veladas artísticas del Teatro Juárez donde un modesto grupo de actores mexicanos luchan por la vida en suelo extraño, haciéndonos conocer a las mas preciadas joyas del teatro contemporáneo en nuestra lengua materna o sea el dulcísimo y sonoro idioma de Cervantes.

Thus the theater became an institution for the preservation of the culture in a foreign environment and for resistance against the influence of the dominant society.

Of course, within the theater house itself, class distinctions were established by price and location of the seating, and if there were any members of the community that could not afford even the modest general admission ticket, touring companies often ended their runs in more modest local establishments in the so-called "barrios pobres." Houses like San Antonio's Teatro Nacional were at the disposition of the community for national celebrations, community-wide fund raisers, or any other special cultural event.

The professional companies also felt responsible for their community as a whole in the United States as well as in Latin America, often donating percentages of the proceeds to establish a clinic or a school in San Antonio, Detroit, New York, or wherever a community was struggling to organize its own life and institutions. Theaters also crusaded to raise funds for flood and earthquake victims in Latin America and for defense committees for unfortunates, like Aurelio Pompa, who were being prosecuted by Anglo-American law. The community in turn showed its appreciation for the individual theatrical artists by showering them with gifts during special benefit performances in their name.

The Great Depression and the forced and voluntary repatriation of Mexicans depopulated not only the communities, but also the theaters.[91] For a while in the 1930's the theatrical artists banded together in such cooperatives as the Compañía de Artistas Unidos and the Compañía Cooperativa in a valiant effort to buy or rent theaters, manage them themselves, and eke out a living. But the economy and the commercial interests of theater owners, who could maximize their own profits by renting films instead of supporting a whole cast, could not sustain their efforts. Those that did not return to Mexico most often continued to pursue their art by organizing non-commercial companies that performed to raise funds for community projects and charities. The stage of artists like Daniel Ferreiro Rea in Los Angeles and Carlos Villalongín in San Antonio was amateurish only in the respect that the artists were not paid. They continued to perform many of the same secular dramas, *zarzuelas*, and *revistas* as before, and did not suddenly switch to religious plays and *pastorelas*, as Brokaw leads us to believe.[92] Through their efforts theater arts were sustained from the 1930's to the 1950's on a voluntary and community basis. A few of the performers, like La Chata Noloesca, were able to prolong their professional careers abroad and in New York where Spanish-language vaudeville survived until the sixties.[93] Others like Leonardo García Astol, followed up their vaudeville career by working in local, Spanish-language radio and television broadcasting after World War II.[94] The tenacious tent theaters also continued their perennial odysseis into the fifties, often setting up right in the camps of migrant farm laborers to perform their *revistas*. It is these traveling theaters that were in part responsible for giving a first exposure of the Hispanic theatrical tradition to some of the young people who would create a Chicano theater in the late sixties.

To summarize briefly, as regards the Hispanic theatrical tradition in the Southwest, the following five points have herein been substantiated and, one would hope, should become a basis for future study: 1) there is a long-standing tradition of Spanish-language professional theater in the Southwest that goes back to at least the mid-nineteenth century; 2) the most important center of activity from the beginning of the tradition until the mid 1930's was Los Angeles, which was also the scene of the greatest flourishing of Spanish-language writing for the stage in the history of the United States; 3) the Los Angeles plays, besides representing commodity theater, also reflected the life, culture and politics of Mexicans in California and the United States; 4) the *revista* genre that was so popular throughout the Southwest was the most important vehicle in reflecting the language, culture and political sentiments of Mexicans; 5) the theater declined as a result of various forces coming to bear at the same time: the Great Depression, voluntary and forced repatriation of Mexicans, the rapid expansion of the talking film industry which could offer inexpensive shows during those economically difficult times.

It should be emphasized that the lights of the professional Hispanic stage were not snuffed out all at once, as Brokaw has asserted, but that they were dimmed over a period of five to six years, beginning with the advent of the economic cataclysm of 1929, during which time impresarios and artists struggled to keep the stage alive, even to the extent of forming cooperatives. Furthermore, after the Hispanic professional stage finally died, theatrical production was not left solely "in the hands of the church and its annual production of *Los pastoreles*." Instead, many of the professional artists put their theater at the service of a wide array of community activities, including raising funds for local religious charities and celebrating patriotic and religious holidays. *Pastorelas* were probably never performed by them, for this is a folk production associated mostly with rural, pastoral communities, not with professionally skilled artists. These artists simply continued to perform the most popular plays from their secular repertoires and only occasionally plays with religious themes. A few of the artists were able to extend their careers in the United States by moving to New York, where Spanish-language vaudeville survived until the early 1960's or by working in local Spanish-language radio and television broadcasting after World War II.[95]

[1]Bonnie Stowell, "Folk Drama Scholarship in the United States: A Selective Survey," *Folklore Annual*, 2 (1970), 51-66.

[2]Juan B. Rael, *The Sources and Diffusion of the Mexican Shepherd's Plays* (Guadalajara: Librería La Joyita, 1965).

[3]Minette Augusta Ker, *The History of the Theater in California in the Nineteenth Century* (Berkeley: University of California Masters Thesis, 1924), p. 5, cites the amateur performance of *Morayma* in 1847 and concludes that for the nineteenth century "The only other amusement of these laughter-loving people somewhat dramatic in form, was the 'maroma'—a Spanish circus."

[4]John E. Englekirk's work, "Notes on the Repertoire of the New Mexican Folktheater," *Southern Folklore Quarterly*, 4/4 (Dec. 1940), 227-237, and "Fernando Calderón en el Teatro Popular Nuevomexicano," *Memoria del Segundo Congreso Internacional de Literatura Iberoamericana* (1941), 227-240, treat the repertoire of small semi-professional troupes as "folktheater."

[5]Jorge Huerta, "Chicano Theater: A Background," *Aztlan*, 2/2 (Fall, 1971), 63-78.

[6]Luis Valdez, "Notes on Chicano Theater," *Chicano Theater One* (Primavera, 1973), p. 7.

[7]For further information on the *pelado* and El Teatro Campesino's *Gran Carpa de la Familia Rascuachi*, see my article in this volume.

[8]For a selected bibliography, see Tina N. Eger, *A Bibliography of Contemporary Chicano Literature* (Berkeley: University of California Chicano Studies Library Publications, 1982).

[9]John W. Brokaw, "Teatro Chicano: Some Reflections," *Educational Theater Journal*, 29/4 (December 1977), p. 538.

[10]*Ibid.*

[11]*Ibid.*, p. 536.

[12]*Ibid.*, p. 540.

[13]*Ibid.*, p. 541.

[14]*Ibid.*

[15]A manuscript copy of *Astucias por heredar un sobrino a un tío*, by Fernando de Reygados, dated 1789, and copied by Mariano Guadalupe Vallejo (1807-1890) for Francisco Rodríguez, was given to Bancroft in 1875. The three-act play from Monterey, California, with stage directions written in the margins (document C-E 120:1) is accompanied by a covering letter (C-E 120:2) that states: "Dicho drama fue el primero que se represento"en California, y en una representación tomaban los soldados que vinieron al país después de la fundación, que llamaban 'los voluntarios de Cataluña.' " The date is, of course, considerably later than 1590

when Farfán's play was performed in El Paso, but it seems that the California performance was followed regularly by others of at least a semi-professional nature, given the practice of townsfolk performing plays by subscription that documentary evidence shows was established by 1847.

¹⁶On the other hand, an editorial published in San Antonio's *Bejareño*, July 19, 1856, seems to indicate that there were no theaters in San Antonio by this date and that, if plays were indeed performed, they would have been performed by amateurs:

> Se nos asegura que varios jóvenes de esta ciudad están haciendo al presente los preparativos necesarios para establecer un nuevo teatro. El número de la población y la falta de diversión pública hace tiempo que reclaman un establecimiento de esa clase; pero dicho sea con verdad nos duele algún tanto ver que se desatiendan algunas mejoras de una necesidad más apremiante y se dé lugar a otras que son secundarias. Nosotros creemos que lo que ha de invertirse en ese teatro, podría dedicarse muy bien a la construcción de un hospital que bien lo necesitan las clases pobres y desvalidos de nuestra ciudad.

During the same year, however, *El Bejareño* noted performances by a "circo mexicano" (June 21 and July 19, 1856). As late as 1884 theatrical performances were still housed at the market place in Laredo, where the Compañía Dramática Mejicana would perform such plays as José Echegaray's *El gran galeoto*, Blasco's *El anzuelo* and short works like *Casa del campo* and *Heraclio y Demócrito* (*El Horizonte*, Dec. 3 and 6, 1884). On July 22, 1891, *El Correo de Laredo* favorably compared the Compañía Hernández' performance of the drama, *Los Mártires de Japón o San Felipe de Jesús* with that of a local Laredo company's performance of *La America en triunfo* at a local tavern for "gente *non sancta.*" The Laredo group was seen as a "compañía raquítica." In 1891 groups of aficionados like the Cuadro Dramático of the Sociedad Hidalgo, directed by Santos Treviño, were still performing such plays as *Los mártires de Tacubaya* at the market place (*El Correo de Laredo*, September 20, 1891).

¹⁷Throughout this period and earlier there is considerable documentation of amateur, folk and religious performances, Vallejo having also mentioned copying a *pastorela* for Bancroft. Alfred Robinson, in *Life in California* (Oakland: Biobooks, 1947), pp. 43-44, described the performance of one at the home of don José Estudillo in San Diego, 1832. But by 1855, sophisticated city-dwellers, probably already accustomed to the polish of the professional stage, were known to snub their noses at the *pastorelas*. One such critic scorned the folk performance as follows in Los Angeles' *El Clamor Público*, December 29, 1855:

> . . . tienen una especie de drama escrito por autores desconocidos, en que imitan *ad libitum* a los antiguos pastores. Algunos trozos son muy enfáticos, pero la mayor parte es una gerigonza ininteligible e insultante. He aquí dos líneas que se repiten más de trescientas veces, es un verdadero *jeux d'esprit*, como dicen los franceses: "Y en palestra literaria,/ Fue mi fortuna varia." Y con esas mismas palabras sigue una retahila ridícula y soez, disparates que sólo cabrían en la imaginación de algún

demente: "Lloren los peces del mar."

By the 1840's the "maromas," or Mexican circuses that performed everything from acrobatics to pantomime and theater, had already reached California, according to Ker, p. 5, and by the late 1850's had reached Arizona, according to Rosemary Gipson, "The Mexican Performers: Pioneer Theater Artists of Tucson," *Journal of Arizona History*, 13/4 (Winter, 1972), p. 236. For a complete history of this circus-theater in Mexico, see Armando de María y Campos, *Los payasos, poetas del pueblo* (Mexico City: Ediciones Botas, 1939).

That the Monterey performance was semi-professional in nature is surmised from the following: 1) it represented one of a series supported by paid subscriptions, and 2) the performance was most likely held in the entertainment establishment of a Monterey merchant, José Abrego (1813-1878), whose son was a cast member. Mr. Abrego was the proprietor of a commercial billiard hall that could have housed theatrical performances. See the José Abrego archive, doc. C-D, 86 v.2, of the Bancroft Collection, which makes reference to his "tienda y junto a ella un salón con dos mesas de villar." On the other hand, strictly amateur performances were usually clearly identified as such, as in the case of the performance of the comedy, *Un novio para la niña*, on June 4, 1865 at the New Almaden Mine by "la compañía de aficionados," *La Voz de México*, June 3, 1865).

[18]According to John Steven McGroarty, *Los Angeles From the Mountains to the Sea*, Vol. 1 (Chicago and New York: The American Historical Society, 1921), p. 378, the great San Francisco operatic tradition begins at this time thanks to Hispanic art and travel by steamship: in 1847 the Alvarez Grand Opera company arrived at the camp of San Francisco from Lima, Peru, lured by a $10,000 subscription. As such it was the first of a long line of opera companies and individual operatic performers that were to travel north from Mexico and Latin America to become part of cities of the United States. The most noteworthy of the individual performers was, of course, José Mojica, who was a leading tenor for the Chicago Lyric Opera in the 1930's and also enjoyed an outstanding cinematic career. Plácido Domingo, is a current example of this tradition.

[19]A promptbook for this unknown play is included in the Hernández-Villalongín archives of the Benson Collection of the University of Texas.

[20]*Diccionario Porrúa de historia, biografía y geografía de México* (Mexico City: Porrúa, 1964), p. 910.

[21]Manuel Mañón, *Historia del Teatro Principal* (Mexico City: Editorial Cultura, 1932), p. 241.

[22]*Ibid.*

[23]Armando de María y Campos, *La dramática mexicana durante el gobierno del Presidente Lerdo de Tejada* (Mexico City: Compañía de Ediciones Populares, 1946), pp. 21-23.

[24]Mañón, p. 241.

[25]Rosemary Gipson, "The Beginning of Theater in Sonora," *Arizona and the West*, 9/4 (Winter, 1967), p. 353.

[26]Mañón, p. 92.

[27]*El Nuevo Mundo*, December 30, 1864.

[28]Exact documentation this far removed in time is impossible. The newspapers that I have used to collect this data often have missing issues and pages. The show on June 30, 1862, is the first performance reported in what has been saved of *La Voz de Méjico*. At this time there is no way to ascertain how far in advance of this date the Estrella Family was performing in San Francisco. We can only hope that other documents come to light. The plays noted in *La Voz de Méjico* were *Fuego del cielo*, March 30, 1862; April 3, the three-act melodrama, *¡Es un angel o Lucha de amor maternal!*; April 5, *La aventura* in four acts by Gertrudis Gómez de Avellaneda; *El prisionero* in two acts and Bretón de los Herreros' *Por poderes*, in one act; April 12, Manuel Bretón de los Herreros' five-act *comedia de costumbres*, *¿Quién es él?*; April 17, Antonio Auset's three-act play, *Trampas inocentes*, and *Por los celos de una monja* in one act; April 24, Victor Hugo's *Angelo, tirano de Padua*; May 1, Tomás Rodríguez Rubí's *Borrascas del corazón!* and the *juguete cómico*, *La ley del embudo*; May 8, Gertrudis Gómez de Avellaneda's drama, *La hija de las flores* and the *juguete*, *Las citas de medianoche*; May 15, Luis Olona's *Las elecciones* and the one-act *Malas tentaciones*; May 22, Olona's two-act comedy *Alza y baja*, and García Gutiérrez' *juguete*, *Un novio al vapor*; August 7 at the Metropolitan Theater, Ventura de la Vega's one-act *¡No hay que tentar al diablo!* and the one-act *Bárbaro y silvestre*.

[29]*La Voz de Méjico*, April 24, 1862.

[30]See *La Voz de Méjico*, September 18 and 20, 1862, and January 1, 1863; also *El Eco del Pacífico*, March 10, 1863.

[31]In *La Voz de Méjico*, June 30, 1863, announcement of the performance, signed Gerardo López del Castillo, the following revealing statement is made:

Invitado por varios de mis amigos y demás personas amantes de las Bellas Artes, y como tal, protectores del ilustrado Arte Dramático, para dar una función de teatro en nuestro hermoso idioma español, no he vacilado un momento en obsequiar sus deseos, sin embargo de los mil inconvenientes con que lucha en este país todo artista español. Al efecto, y aprovechando la oportunidad de la llegada a este puerto por el vapor "Orizava" del artista mexicano, D. José, de Jesús Díaz, he arreglado para la noche de este día un escogido espectáculo. . . .

[32]The fragmented record of *La Voz de Méjico* notes only the following performances: July 5, 1863, Tomás Rodríguez Rubí's four-act drama, *La trenza de sus cabellos*, and the *juguete cómico*, *Cuerpo y sombra*; July 26, the three-act *Flor de un día*, by Francisco Camprodón, and *Bárbaro y silvestre* again; August 26, Part II of Camprodón's *Flor de un día*, *Espinas de una flor*, in three acts.

[33]See *El Nuevo Mundo*, December 30, 1864, and for the story on López del Castillo's benefit performance at which Joe Murphy and Walter Bray's minstrels played, see *El Nuevo Mundo*, December 7, 1864.

[34]At least two other professional companies were performing in the San Francisco area at this time. According to *La Voz de Méjico*, July 9, 1864, the Compañía Salazar performed *Vivir loco y morir más* and *El puñal del godo*, by Zorrilla at Tucker's Academy. *La Voz del Nuevo Mundo* followed the Compañía Española

de Drama, Canto y Baile de Mariano Luque, rather closely, noting on June 16, 1864, the performance of Juan Polán y Coll's *La campana de la Almudaina* in three acts and the *sainete*, *Casa del campo*; and on June 17, *La campana* in two acts and *Maruja* at the Opera House on Bush Street. The newspaper states that the company performs a different play every night, with an additional play on Saturdays. Unfortunately the issues from June 17 until July 17, 1864, are missing. We hear of the Luque company again on July 17, 1864, now at the Teatro California. On July 19, *La cabaña de Tom*, translated by Ramón Saavedra, and the *juguete*, *Los parvalillos* were performed and on September 27 now at Maguire's Theater, *El terremoto de la Martinica*, in four acts, and the one-act *zarzuela*, *La castañera*.

[35]María y Campos, pp. 21-22.

[36]Rodolfo Usigli, *Mexico in the Theater* (University of Mississippi: Romance Monographs, 1976), p. 102.

[37]María y Campos, p. 46.

[38]*Ibid.*, pp. 22-23.

[39]According to *La Crónica*, April 3, 1878, the Teatro Alarcón's impresarios were Señores Guerrero and Vásquez and Professor Velazco was the director of the orchestra.

[40]*La Voz de Méjico*, April 24, 1862, mentions the Familia Maiquez company as performing in Los Angeles.

[41]Another troupe, Señores Romero y Compañía, was noted by *La Crónica*, April 3, 1878, as performing Zorrilla's *Los dos virreyes de Nápoles* and the sainete, *Me conviene esta mujer*. Members of the troupe were Adelina Domínguez, señores Romero, Angulo, Pozo and Franco. On February 25, 1882, *La Voz del Nuevo Mundo* reported a performance of *La cabaña de Tom* by the Compañía Dramática Jay Rial (perhaps this is an English-Speaking company) and on April 7, 1883, anticipated the use of the Tivoli Theater once or twice a week for a series of *zarzuelas*.

[42]See Gipson, "The Mexican Performers," pp. 235-252.

[43]The remainder of the performances noted in *La Crónica* were: March 12, Juan de Ariza's three-act historical drama, *Antonio de Leiva o la gran batallón de Pavia* and the short piece, *Amar sin dejarse amar*; March 19, Luis M. de Larra's *comedia de costumbres*, *Oros, copas, espadas y bastos* and the short piece, *Pescar y cazar*; March 26, the religious drama, *El cura de aldea*, by Enrique Pérez Escrich, and the one-act *Don Ramón*; on Saturday April 15, the first four acts of Zorrilla's *Don Juan Tenorio* and on the 16th, the second three acts, as well as the one-act, *Tres eran tres las hijas de Elena*; April 23, a repeat of the 16th; April 30, Narciso Serro's three-act drama, *El reloj de San Plácido o la mujer enterrada en vida*, and *El loco por fuerza* in one act; May 5, "función patriótica," the three-act *comedia*, *Quevedo y la buñolera o poderoso caballero es Don Dinero*; May 10, Ventura de la Vega's drama, *Arturo o el amor de madre*, and the short piece, E.H. (with Señora Mollá from the Compañía Mollá playing the role of the *gracioso*); May 21, Eduardo Zamora y Caballero's *El filósofo del gran mundo o una coqueta del día*; May 28, Enrique Zumel's *comedia de costumbres* in three acts, *Riendas del gobierno*, and the one-act *El tigre de Bengala* in which some local amateurs

were allowed to participate; May 31, (under the directorship of Pedro C. de Pellón from now on), Palau y Coll's *La Campana de la almudaina o el toque de agonía*, with the *zarzuela, La viuda y el sacristán*; June 10, the drama, *Viva la libertad*, and the short *La casa del campo*; June 18, *El castillo de Balsain o el rey vencido*, by Manuel Tamayo and Luis Fernández Guerra, and a a repetition of *La casa del campo*; July 1, the drama, *La oración de la tarde*, and the *juguete cómico*, *No lo quiero saber*.

44Gipson, "The Mexican Performers," p. 243.

45Including Zumel's *Viva la libertad* and *Amar sin dejarse amar*, according to Gipson, "The Mexican Performers," p. 245.

46*Ibid.*, p. 241.

47"Por la carta que tenemos a la vista sabemos que la Compañía Mollá se halla actualmente en Guaymas habiendo salido de Hermosillo para ese lugar la semana pasada."

48The following plays were performed: June 3, 1876, *Los soldados de plomo*, by Eduardo Equilaz, and the *sainete, Las gracias de Gedeón*; June 24, Luis Mariano de Larra's *comedia de costumbres* in three acts, *El amor y el interés and* the short *Potencia a potencia*; July 8, *Flores y perlas*; July 15, *Los soldados de plomo*; October 28, Larra's four-act play, *Bienaventurados los que lloran*, and the short *No más secreto*; December 23, Larra's *La cosecha o el fruto del libertinaje* and the *zarzuela, Geroma la castañera*; December 30, Gaspar Núñez de Arce's *Deudas de la honra* and the one-act *La sospecha*; March 7, 1877, Zorrilla's three-act *Traidor, inconfeso y mártir*.

49April 7, 1877, Antonio Guillén y Sánchez' *Malditas sean las mujeres*; April 14, the same; June 2, Gaspar Núñez de Arce's *Deudas de la honra*; May 26, 1883, the same plus the one-act *Como el pez en el agua*; June 6, Bretón de los Herreros' *El poeta y la beneficiada o una vieja como hay muchas* and *Pescar y cazar*; June 16, Pastorndo's five-act drama, *Las dos madres*; June 30, Echegaray's *La esposa del vengador*; July 21, two one-act plays, *No hay humo sin fuego* and *Me conviene esta mujer*; August 11, José María Tovar's *La vuelta del mundo o un episodio de la independencia*; Larra's *Los dos lazos de la familia* and *Me conviene esta mujer*, on January 1, 1884; January 2, *La esposa del vengador*.

50Between 1900 and 1930, many of the smaller cities and towns along the route supported their own Spanish-language theater houses. I have herein compiled a preliminary listing. In Texas: Teatro Casino in Eagle Pass, Teatro Estrella and Salón Hidalgo in Brownsville, Teatro Juárez in San Benito, Teatro Casino in Del Rio, Teatro Melva in Corpus Christi, Teatro Mercedes in Mercedes, Teatro Chapultepec in East Donna, Teatro Nacional in Weslaco, Teatro Atenas in Kingsville. In New Mexico: Teatro Juárez in Las Cruces, Salón La Joya in La Joya, Salón Alianza Hispano Americana and Salón A. C. Torres in Socorro. In Arizona: Teatro Juárez in Sonora Town, Teatro Royal in Nogales, Teatro Mexicano in Superior, Teatro Amazu in Phoenix, Teatro Yuma in Yuma. In California: Teatro México in Brawley, Teatro México in Maravilla Park, Teatro Centenario in Ensenada, Teatro Salón in Santa Monica, Teatro Bonito in Belvedere, Club Hispano Americano in Pittsburgh, and many others.

[51]My informant, Mr. Leonardo García Astol, performed along the Rio Grande Valley during the late teens and the 1920's with his father's Compañía Azteca, after having performed in the interior of Mexico during the hostilities of the Mexican Revolution. Touring to the small towns on both sides of the border was called "puebleando." Mr. Astol also informed me that he eventually formed his own company and settled in San Antonio, where he still resides, to perform repertory and, later in the 1930's, vaudeville at the Teatro Nacional. He also performed as a "peladito" at the head of a company in Los Angeles during the 1930's.

[52]By 1910, Laredo supported four fiercely competetive theater houses: Teatro Eléctrico, Teatro Dreamland, Teatro Alarcón and Teatro Solórzano. When a major company was not performing at one of these, it would feature *sainetes, zarzuelas,* couplets and variety acts in between showings of silent films. According to the Laredo newspaper, *La Crónica*, December 14, 1911, the Teatro Eléctrico employed its own repertory company made up of local artists. They performed the following *zarzuelas*: *La marcha de Cadiz, Los camarones, Chin chun chan, El bateo* and *La banda de trompetas.* The Teatro Solórzano, on the other hand, varied its fare by offering "dramas y comedias los sábados, domingos y jueves, juguetes cómicos el resto de la semana," (*La Crónica,* Dec. 14, 1911). During the next twenty years, the doors to other Spanish-language theaters would open here: Teatro Iris, Teatro García, Teatro Strand, Teatro Independencia, Teatro Variedades, Teatro Iturbide, Teatro Nacional.

[53]See my article, "Mexican Theater in a Midwest Industrial City." *Latin American Theater Review* 7/1 (Fall, 1973), p. 43-48.

[54]Los Angeles' *El Heraldo de México*, September 16, 1924, announced the arrival of La Compañía Hispano-Mexicana de Zarzuela y Variedades F. Díaz de León from three seasons of performances in New York and a tour that included Philadelphia, Chicago, Cleveland, Detroit and other points. San Antonio's *La Prensa*, January 1, 1924, noted the following about the company's performances in Detroit:

> No obstante la crueldad del invierno los hispano-americanos concurren diariamente a las funciones que ofrece la Compañía Díaz de León, ya que muy rara vez se presenta la oportunidad a esas colonias de presenciar espectáculos en que se representan sus costumbres y en que toman parte actores de su misma raza.

A complete itinerary of Spain's Compañía María Guerrero y Fernando Díaz de Mendoza was published in San Antonio's *La Prensa*, November 21, 1926. It included the following: January 5 and 6, Jerusalem Temple, New Orleans; January 8, Houston Auditorium; January 9, Municipal Auditorium, San Antonio; January 12, Grand Theater, Douglas; January 14, Shrine Temple, Phoenix; January 15, San Bernardino Auditorium; the week of January 16, Mason Opera House, Los Angeles; the week of January 23, Columbia Theater, San Francisco; then from San Francisco to San Diego, El Paso, St. Louis, Chicago, Detroit, Canton, Pittsburg, Philadelphia and New York. Virginia Fábregas' many tours often extended to the outer reaches of the Spanish-speaking world, not just North America. *La Prensa*, December 1, 1926, supplied the following itinerary: San Antonio, El

Paso, Los Angeles, San Francisco, Philippines, Spain, Canary Islands, Puerto Rico, Cuba and Mexico.

[55]One former member of the Fábregas company was Agustín Molinari, who died in the United States in 1934 and was succeeded on the stage here by his children, Raquel, Juan and Agustín, all of whom took part in a benefit performance to raise funds for his grave stone on October 15, 1934 at the Teatro Hidalgo in Los Angeles (*La Opinión*, October 10, 1934). Bernardo Fougá, noted as a member of the Fábregas company in Puerto Rico in 1912 by Emilio J. Pasarell, *Orígenes y desarrollo de la afición teatral en Puerto Rico—Siglo XX* (Río Piedras: Editorial Universitaria, 1967) p. 45, became an important director on the San Antonio stage and during the Depression was responsible for conducting charitable performances there at the head of the Club Dramático of the Inmaculado Corazón de María church. It is important to note that the plays produced were the same secular plays of his professional career: *El talento de mi mujer*, by Antonio Paso and Francisco Pacheco (*La Prensa*, February 23, 1932); *Papá la Bonnard*, by Jean Alcord (*La Prensa*, February 24, 1932); *El juramento de la primorosa* (*La Prensa*, October 23, 1932); *La mujer adúltera* (*La Prensa*, December 1, 1932); *El orgullo de Albacete*, by Joaquín Abati and Antonio Paso (*La Prensa*, January 29, 1933); etc. This was also true of Manuel Cotera, who first came to San Antonio in 1916 with the María Martínez company. By 1921 he had formed his own Compañía Cómico Lírico Dramático in the Alamo City (*La Prensa*, January 16, 1921) and for more than ten years continued to perform throughout central Texas. During the Depression he too directed charitable performances on a regular basis.

[56]In Southwestern newspapers there are occasional references to formalized theatrical circuits like "el circuito Hipodrome" (*Hispano Americano*, San Francisco, April 1919); "el circuito Chataqua" that contracted Los Hermanos Llera, a vaudeville singing act for 125 performances across the United States (*La Prensa*, San Antonio, December 10, 1925); "el circuito Interstate" (*La Prensa*, October 3, 1924), and New York agent Walter O. Llndsay who booked the Compañía María Guerrero from New York to Los Angeles and back via New Orleans and the Southwest as a trial run for other national tours by Hispanic companies that he would manage (*La Prensa*, November 21, 1926).

[57]For instance, singer-actress Nelly Fernández toured throughout Canada and the United States with other Mexican acts. For a time she was under contract to the Pantages vaudeville circuit for as much as $1,000 per month (*La Opinión*, August 8, 1933).

[58]*La Opinión*, Los Angeles, April 11, 1932.

[59]San Antonio's most important house was the Teatro Nacional built in 1917 and owned by Sam Lucchese, also owner of the Zendejas. Other San Antonio theaters were the Aurora, Texas, Obrero, Azteca, Hidalgo, Zaragoza, Princess, Union, Amigos del Pueblo, Salón Casino, Beethoven Hall, Majestic, Municipal Auditorium, Progreso, Palace, Teatro Salón San Fernando, Juárez, State.

[60]These were the Metropolitan, Cabaret Sanromán, Lyceum Hall, Empress, Leo Carrillo, Orange Grove, Mason, Million Dollar, Major, Paramount, Figueroa Playhouse, Alcázar, Philharmonic Auditorium and Unique.

[61]It was often repeated in the newspapers that the Hispanic Theaters drew their largest crowds every time they featured plays by local writers. For instance, Gabriel Navarro wrote in *La Opinión*, April 12, 1930, that the largest profits of 1929 were made at the Teatro México from local plays. Nevertheless, as popular as these plays may have been, business interests at times worked against their production and against the playwrights' reaping the benefits of their craft. According to Esteban V. Escalante, *La Opinión*, April 20, 1930, the writer's 25% share of the opening-day box office—which often amounted to $100 to $150—led impresarios to jealously limit the author's payment to a flat fee of $20 or $30 or simply to eliminate local plays and produce instead well-worn *obras* ("españolas o chichimecas") for which they did not have to pay a dime.

[62]For instance, by its eighth performance, Adalberto Elías González' *Los amores de Ramona* had attracted 15,000 people to the Teatro México (*El Heraldo de México*, November 24, 1927).

[63]For instance, *La Opinión*, August 12, 1933, reports: De México se nos escribe diciendo que para el mes de septiembre próximo, se estrenará en uno de los teatros de aquella capital, una revista con libreto del autor teatral Esteban V. Escalante, muy conocido en nuestros círculos por haber vivido muchos años en Los Angeles. La revista, se asegura, tendrá como motivo la vida de los mexicanos en el extranjero teniendo un cuadro dedicado exclusivamente a Hollywood.

[64]A journalist for *La Opinión*, Miguel Arce, whose novel *Ladrona* was also published by *La Opinión*'s publishing house and was later adapted for the stage; Brígido Caro, journalist for *El Heraldo de México* and author of *La gloria de la raza*, *El Niño Fidencio*, *Joaquín Murrieta* and *México y Estados Unidos* (according to Francisco Monterde, *Bibliografía del teatro en México*, Mexico: Monografías Bibliográficas Mexicanas, 1933, p.95, Caro was also author of *Heraclio Bernal o el rey de los bandidos*, published in Alamos, Mexico, 1894); Alfredo Busson, who died in Los Angeles on December 18, 1929, was a journalist and author of *La vendetta* and the arrangements for two *revistas*, *Su Majestad Tiraklán* and *Ya mi' anda*; Antonio Mediz Bolio is reported as having finished his play, *El sol de la humanidad*, in Los Angeles and debuted it at the Teatro Novel, where his socialist drama, *La ola*, was also produced, according to *El Heraldo de México*, June 6 and June 22, 1920; according to *El Heraldo de México*, June 9, 1926, the Teatro Hidalgo was going to contract Jorge Loyo, a writer for Mexico City's *El Universal Ilustrado*, to write a series of *revistas*; José Gou Bourgell, a Spanish journalist and author of *El suicida*, *Virginidades* and *El crimen de la virtud*; Raúl Castell, who often collaborated with the famed Mexican composer, Ernesto González Jiménez, to write *revistas* such as *El mundo de las pelonas*, *El Tenorio en California*, *En el país del shimmy*; Max Cervantes, author of the drama, *El puñal del yaqui*; Arturo Chacel, author of *Se solicita un marido*; Juan N. Chavarri, author of *Cuando ellas sean ellos*; Agustín Haroy T., Editor of Los Angeles' *La Prensa* and and author of *EL proceso del mal humor* and *El gran recurso*; Margarita Robles, founder and director of a school for Mexicans in in Los Angeles and author of *Corazon Ciego*; Pezantes Ganoza, a Peruvian writer and author of *La sinfonía incompleta*, *Media noche*, and *El coyote*; Daniel L. Cosío, author of *El*

*porqué de nuestras guerras*; Ramón Méndez del Río, also a Mexican journalist and author of *Los repatriados*; Antonio Helú, novelist, Hollywood screenwriter and author of *Los mexicanos se van*, *Esta noche me emborracho*, *La coartada*, *Los cuatro náufragos*, *La ciudad de los temblores* (with Jesús Segovia), *El gangster* and *El hambre que todo lo arreglaba* (Monterde, p. 180, notes that his play, *La comedia termina*, was published in Mexico in 1928); José Sandozequi and Hernán Sandozequi, father and son writing team for the Compañía Arte Moderno, were authors of many short works including *El mundo de las locas*, *Los sueños de Nerón*, *La aventura de María Elena*, *Llama un taxi*, *Espíritus de alquimia*, *Los Angeles en el infierno* and *El libro de oro de Hollywood*; María de Jesús Olazábal, also a journalist for *La Opinión* and author of *El presunto suicida*; Gustavo Solano, a Salvadoran who used the pen name "Conde Gris" in his newspaper columns, was contracted in 1927 by el Teatro Principal to write one *revista* per week (*El Heraldo de México*, August 28, 1927) and by the Teatro Hidalgo in 1926 to provide a series of works "de ambiente local" (*El Heraldo de México*, September 2, 1926), was author of *Mexico glorioso y trágico*, *La gran sorpresa*, *La casa de Birján*, *Al enfermo lo que pida*, *Las falsas apariencias* and many others; Daniel Venegas, known as "El Malcriado" in his newspaper columns, was author of *Nuestro egoísmo*, *Quién es el culpable* and *revistas* such as *El con-su-la-do*, *El Maldito Jazz*, *Revista astronómica* and *El establo de de Arizmendi* (in honor of the boxer Baby Arizmendi).

[65]A few of the most productive and popular authors of *revistas* were: Don Catarino, los Sandozequi, and Guz Aguila (Antonio Guzmán Aguilera). Guzmán Aguilera, famous in Mexico as an *autor de revistas*, held the distinction of being under contract to the Teatro Hidalgo in Los Angeles for the extraordinary fee of $1,000 per month (*La Opinión*, August 8, 1933).

[66]*La Opinión*, December 25, 1924.

[67]*El Heraldo de México*, July 21, 1924.

[68]According to *El Heraldo de México*, April 29, 1927, this piece was a response to certain anti Mexican statements made by President Calvin Coolidge.

[69]*El Heraldo de México*, October 13, 1927.

[70]*El Heraldo de México*, October 8, 1927.

[71]*El Heraldo de México*, August 25, 1923.

[72]It is in the *revistas* that we find a great deal of humor based on culture shock typically derived from following the misadventures of a naive, recent immigrant from Mexico who has difficulty getting accustomed to life in the big Anglo-American metropolis. A plot summary of Romualdo Tirado's *De México a Los Angeles*, published in *El Heraldo de México*, November 28, 1920, gives a good idea of an early example of this immigrant-type comedy:

> Un sastre, establecido en la capital de México, ya entrado en años, ha oído hablar frecuentemente de las grandezas y adelantos de los Estados Unidos, y en especial (porque es lo que a él le interesa) lo referente a su oficio. Entusiasmado por las fabulosas noticias que recibe, y ambicionando aprender y hasta hacerse rico, se viene a los Estados Unidos, sin más compañía que una pequeña libreta en la que alguien apuntó al-

gunas frases en inglés, con lo que él cree estar al cabo de la calle en cuanto a la ignorancia del idioma; pero resulta que desde el mismo momento en que llega, se convence de que el librito de marras no le sirve de nada y después de recibir varias hostiles manifestaciones de parte de unos 'primos', un gendarme de quien el hace el panegírico, comparándolo con nuestros polizontes, se lo lleva a rastras y lo mete en un hotel donde sigue pasando la pena negra, por no poder hacerse entender. Por fin llega a un restaurante mexicano (?) donde cree estar a salvo de molestias y resulta que le dan un tremendo golpe con el timo de la 'indemnizacion' que le obligan a pagar a un individuo norteamericano a cuya esposa ha invitado a un modesto 'ice cream soda'. Va nuestro héroe a Venice, y se encanta; pero a pesar de todo, más impresionado por lo desagradable de sus chascos que por la belleza de la playa, decide regresar a México, sin haber aprendido siquiera un sistema nuevo de ensartar agujas.

Later on in the decade, when the Depression and repatriation take hold, the theme of culture shock is converted to one of outright cultural conflict, especially in dramas based on early California history.

[73]*El Heraldo de México*, July 31, 1926, reports on its financial success, as well as on the number of performances.

[74]The Cuadro de Aficionados "Junípero Serra" performed this play as a benefit, fund raiser for the Alianza Hispano-Americana, according to *El Heraldo de México*, December 27, 1927.

[75]Other plays by Eduardo Carillo, who came to Los Angeles in the early twenties as an actor in María Teresa Montoya's Company (*La Opinión*, August 8, 1933), are *Los hombres desnudos*, *Heraclio Bernal o el Rayo de Sinaloa*, *El zarco* and *Patria y honor*; his *revistas* and *zarzuelas* include *Los Angeles al día*, *Malditos sean los hombres*, *Su majestad la carne*, *Eva triunfadora*, and *En las puertas del infierno*.

[76]Tomas Ybarra-Frausto, "El Teatro Libertad: Antecedents and Actuality," *Teatro Libertad* (Tuscon: Teatro Libertad, 1978), p. xiv, reports on his interview of Marcos Glodel, a former actor, who remembered that his company, Cuadro México-España, would enter the audience after performances of this play to collect signatures on petitions to the governor of California for redress of the injustices perpetrated against Pompa. It seems that this was not an isolated practice; the Circo Escalante Hermanos Compañía de Baile y Variedades, which presented *zarzuela* and variety and circus acts, gave a benefit performance in March, 1927, in efforts to raise funds in Phoenix for the defense of Alfredo Grijalva, accused of murdering an American official. See the Escalante broadside in the Manuel Gamio "Folkloric Materials" file of the Bancroft Collection. Regardless of the use of *El proceso de Aurelio Pompa*, or any other play, for raising defense funds, it is important to note that plays based on topics like the struggle of Aurelio Pompa were commodities that the Los Angeles audiences consumed for the human drama, relevance, and even sensationalism that they promised. In fact, after Aurelio Pompa was executed— this too was incorporated into the play—Carrillo's play continued to be financially successful, so much so that a drama critic from *El*

*Heraldo de México*, December 2, 1925, editorialized that the dead should be left to rest and that impresarios should not be so greedy for profits at the expense of the deceased:

> La empresa del Hidalgo, sacrificando sus intereses pecuniarios, por humanidad y respeto a la raza, debe abstenerse de que el cuadro de artistas que allí actúa, represente "obras" como la que se refiere al infeliz mexicano que, aún en la tumba debe estar sufriendo cada vez que se ve caracterizado por uno de los faranduleros de la calle Main. . . .

[77]*La vida de amor de Rodolfo Valentino*, *Las incomprensibles*, *La cuerda floja*, *Sangre de tigre*, *La pura verdad*, *Al fin solos*, *Un beso en las tinieblas*, *La muerte*, *Tres piedras*, *La que lo amó locamente*, *Las mariposas de Hollywood* and *La agonía de un sueño*.

[78]His *revistas* and short pieces are *Los Angeles al día* (in collaboration with Eduardo Carrillo), *La ciudad de irás y no volverás*, *La ciudad de los extras*, *Su excelencia el amor*, *México quiere paz* (apropósito cómico-lírico), *La maldita guerra* (zarzuela), *El gran vivir*, *Loco amor*, *El proceso de Los Angeles*, *Las luces de Los Angeles*, *Los Angeles en pijama* and *Revista de radio 1934*.

[79]Other dramas by Navarro are *Cuando entraron los dorados*, *Alma yaqui*, *La señorita Estela* (after his novel by the same title) and *La Venganza*.

[80]Not only did Virginia Fábregas make arrangements to buy the rights of González' works, and she did actually produce them, but it seems she never paid the author for his works. This led him to threaten to sue her for her usurpation and for even ascribing his play, *Ramona*, to a fictitious Italian writer, Alfredo D. Cavaletti. See *La Opinión*, January 12, 1920.

[81]The first version of his play, *Sangre yaqui*, opened at the Capitol Theater, *El Heraldo de México*, October 22, 1926.

[82]According to *El Heraldo de México*, October 27, 1927, *La degradación de los pobres* was translated into English by an American writer.

[83]*El Heraldo de México*, June 9, 1927.

[84]So popular was *Ramona* that composer L. Mendoza López offered to buy the rights and tour it throughout Mexico as a *zarzuela* with music that he would write for it. See *El Heraldo de México*, January 1, 1929.

[85]*El Heraldo de México*, October 14, 1923.

[86]He also published a novel by the same title in 1923.

[87]Monterde, *Bibliografía*, p. 163, shows that this play was published by the Sonora Printing Company in 1929.

[88]See Armando María y Campos, *El teatro de género chico en la Revolución Mexicana* (México: Biblioteca del Instituto Nacional de Estudios Históricos de la Revolución Mexicana, 1956), for a discussion and history of the *revista* as a genuine Mexican theatrical form. Especially interesting is his discussion of the *revista política* as a libretto that was written for social and political commentary during the Mexican Revolution, pp. 164-171. *Revistas* later degenerated into a loose format for comedy and musical performance in which the *pelado*, or underdog character, often improvised a substantial part of his role. Nevertheless, as a literary form, the *revista* was cultivated throughout the 1920's and 30's in Los

Angeles, as it was in Mexico. Antonio Magaña Esquivel and Ruth S. Lamb, *Breve historia del teatro mexicano* (México: Ediciones de Andrea, 1958), p. 99 also emphasize the importance of the authors of *revista* librettoes.

[89]*La Opinión*, June 13, 1932. The other side of the repatriation story, how the expatriates returning to Mexico fared in their homeland, was also dramatized in such works as Juan Bustillos Oro's three-act epic, *Los que vuelven* (*La Opinión*, February 27, 1932).

[90]Fidel Murillo, "Teatrales," *La Opinión*, November 20, 1930.

[91]Fidel Murillo, theater critic for *La Opinión*, in the August 8, 1934 edition, tried to weigh the various factors (Depression, repatriation, summer heat, competition from the cheap American movies and variety shows, acculturation) that were thought to have contributed to the decline of the theater movement:

Estremece pensar en la verdad. Lo que falta es el público. Hace unos cuantos años, bastaba cualquier incentivo minúsculo para arrastrar a las multitudes a los salones de espectáculos. Tres llenos, en sábado, domingo y lunes, eran de cajón. Los demas días, cuando se les reforzaba con alguna atracción, o un estreno cualquiera, se defendían decorosamente. Ahora, ni con grandes atracciones—a no ser que se trate de José Mojica, de Dolores del Río o de Lupe Vélez—se puede llenar el teatro. Las excusas que se dan son las del calor, la mala situación económica de la colonia, etc. La verdad desnuda, desagradable como todas las verdades que hieren, es la asentada antes: que ya no hay público para nuestros teatros.

Y es que desde hace algún tiempo, han estado saliendo de retorno a México, grandes corrientes de repatriados, oficial o privadamente. Quedan en Los Angeles las familias que no han podido abandonar la ciudad o las que no han querido hacerlo. Aquéllas, piensan más en resolver el problema del momento, que en divertirse. Estas, prefieren francamente el espectáculo americano.

Los viejos son pocos. Los jóvenes han aprendido inglés, y se encuentran con que un teatro de primera les ofrece variedades de primera también, más película, orquesta, etc., por una cantidad ínfima, algo que no pueden hacer nuestros teatros, que no cuentan con más patrocinio que el de la colonia de habla española local.

[92]See John W. Brokaw, "A Mexican-American Acting Company, 1849-1939," *Educational Theater Journal* 27/1 (March, 1975), p. 23-29.

[93]See John C. Miller, "Hispanic Theater in New York, 1965-1977," *Revista Chicano-Riqueña* 6/1 (Winter, 1978), p. 40-59.

[94]Astol even wrote and produced plays in Spanish for a local San Antonio television station during the 1950's.

[95]I would like to express my appreciation to the National Endowment for the Humanities summer grants program which made possible some of my research for this study, as well as offer special thanks to Oscar Treviño and Richard Chabrán, Chicano Studies Librarians at the University of California, for their invaluable assistance.

# The Mexican Stage in the Southwestern United States as a Sounding Board for Cultural Conflict

As I have shown elsewhere, the Mexican/Hispanic professional theatre in the Southwest dates back to the mid-nineteenth century.[1] It is my thesis that from its origins up to the present day, the Mexican/Hispanic theatre, besides serving esthetic and entertainment needs, also served the social and political purposes of the community, which conceived of itself at different times as a conquered people whose culture was threatened, later as a colony in exile ("México de afuera"), and today as a minority oppressed by a larger, monolithic culture.

One writer, Brokaw, has questioned the reality of political motivation for the theatre of the past. Writing in 1977, he categorized as "mythology" the belief that today's *teatros*, like El Teatro Campesino, which "cleaves to certain social and political issues which date back at least to the Anglo occupation,"[2] are more or less continuing the tradition of a resident theatre. According to Brokaw, "controversial subjects, therefore, had no place in such enterprises," i.e., Mexican theatre in the Southwest. "When Mexican affairs were mentioned in the plays, it was invariably in terms of political celebration." (Brokaw, p. 538). It was Chicanos, according to Brokaw, who began to use theatre for a political purpose. In the late 1920s, "The teatros ceased and theatrical production in the Spanish language was left in the hands of the Church and its annual productions of *Los pastoreles* [sic]. There it remained until the Chicanos of the 1960s decided that drama had a function to fulfill in their scheme of things." (Brokaw, p. 540).

Brokaw does not take into account the nature of the audiences that attended the shows in question, nor the social, political and cultural environment of the Mexican colonies during the period which he studies, i.e., the 1880s through the 1920s. On the other hand, judging from documentary evidence in newspapers, I have observed that the special social and political relations of the stage to the Mexican community begin to take shape very early. Of the ten or so resident theatrical companies that were performing in California during the 1860s, the company directed by the great Mexican actor, Gerardo López del Castillo (Compañía Dramática Española) may serve as an early example of the special relationship that Mexican and Hispanic theatres would always maintain with their communities in the United States.

First of all, the Company's director, Gerardo López del Castillo, was an intensely patriotic individual who fought against Maximilian and, after returning to Mexico following his residence in California, became known as a tireless promoter of a Mexican national theatre. In San Francisco, López del Castillo served as the very active president of the Sociedades Patrióticas Mexicanas. At all times, his patriotic activities, his acting and his speeches—the latter were published in the San Francisco newspaper, *El Eco del Pacífico*[3]—were considered as the finest example of the Spanish language and as furthering the preservation of Mexican and Hispanic culture in an alien environment.

At all times the Compañía Dramática Española was available to the community for benefits and fundraisers. In fact, one of the most important causes that was supported by its performances was the raising of funds for Juárez' army; after the war, funds were also raised for the widows and orphans produced by the war.

Finally it is important to note that companies like the Compañía Dramática Española served the Hispanic community at large, not just the elite, but the grass roots as well. This fact is illustrated by the defense of the grass roots audience made by a *La Voz de Méjico* critic writing in 1862 when a writer for the French-language newspaper, *Le Phare*, penned "injurias e insultos a todo un público . . . Si algunos vaqueros descubrio "el Sr.del Phare en la reunión y si tal oficio le parece bajo, el trabajo es en América el mejor título que se puede tener al respeto general . . ."[4]

Along those lines, as far as the theatre appealing to broad sectors of the society and its producers having political and social motivation, there is an earlier example. The theatre house in Monterey, California, was the billiard hall in José Abrego's Inn, and there is ample evidence that the performances of Spanish-language melodrama by subscription were attended by both Spanish and English speakers.[5] In an 1847 fire at the inn, four hundred volunteers of the Stevenson Regiment came to the rescue and stole everything from Abrego. During the process, they discovered barrels of lead for bullets.[6] It is very possible that Abrego was an insurgent!

By the turn of the century, companies were touring throughout the Southwest. But the rapid expansion and boom of the Spanish-language stage really began with the massive immigration that took place during the Mexican Revolution. Theatres became the primary cultural and entertainment institutions for Mexican and Mexican American families alike. Following the initiative of elites who came as religious and political refugees of the Revolution, the theatres became an integral part of the concept of "colonia mexicana en el exilio" or "el México de afuera." As such, theatrical performances in the Spanish language were seen as preserving the language, customs and mores of transplanted Mexicans and culturally oppressed Mexican Americans. The theatre further offered clean and healthy entertainment for the whole family in contrast to what was considered as the looser morality of Anglo-American diversions.

In the April 26, 1916, edition of San Antonio's *La Prensa*, a critic commented on the importance of the theatre in this regard. For the community, the Spanish-language stage was ". . . un espectáculo verdaderamente artístico, culto moralizador. Por otra parte puede considerarse como una obra patriótica y de solidaridad de raza, el concurrir a las veladas artísticas del teatro Juárez donde un modesto grupo de actores mexicanos luchan por la vida en suelo extraño, haciéndonos conocer las más preciadas joyas del teatro contempor neo en nuestra lengua materna o sea el dulcísimo y sonoro idioma de Cervantes."

On February 23, 1918, *La Prensa de Los Angeles* justified the construction of the Teatro Hidalgo as follows: "En esta ciudad se hacía sentir ya la imperiosa necesidad de tener espectáculo de alta cultura y moralidad en nuestro idioma."

The June 1, 1919, issue of San Antonio's *La Prensa* gave the following reason for the Sociedad de la Unión's construction of a theatre: "levantar el concepto que nuestra raza tiene en el extranjero." And, indeed, the sale of bonds for the construction of the theatre was highly promoted as patriotic. What is evident from the three quotes, is the patriotism and "solidaridad de la raza," as well as the reinforcement of Cervantes' sweet and sonorous language, and that the community felt that its culture was threatened and that the theatre had a definite role to play in its protection and survival.

Even attendance at the more modest Mexican circuses and tent shows was a motive for nationalism. In the December 16, 1917, edition of Los Angeles' *El Heraldo de México*, the public was exhorted to attend the Escalante Circus in this manner: "Si usted no ha ido al circo, dispóngase a hacerlo hoy mismo, no olvidando que se trata de un espectáculo mexicano que en muchos sentidos, como en arroyo y limpieza de sus actos, es superior a los grandes circos americanos." Once again the looser morality of Anglo-American entertainments, besides language and nationality was in question.

And as the stage declined during the Depression and the great repatriations which devastated theatre audiences, theatre critics made last-ditch appeals to the nationalism of Mexicans and the need to protect the culture.

"Necesitamos teatro . . . siquiera sea para contrarrestar la influencia de letras, costumbres y tendencias sajonas que nos envuelven por momentos," decried Los Angeles' *La Opinión*.[7] The same newspaper also appealed for the community to support struggling companies of actors: ". . . todos son nacidos y educados en México, entusiastas de la conservación de la cultura hispana que ellos adquirieron, y unidos por la necesidad artística de contrarrestar la influencia del teatro extraño a nuestras tendencias, nuestra tradición y nuestras costumbres."[8] In 1931 another *Opinión* writer promoted theatrical attendance "por amor a nuestra cultura agonizante."[9]

But during the heyday of the Mexican/Hispanic stage in California, the culture was far from agonizing. Eight major theatre houses kept their stages busy during the 1920s offering everything from Spanish melodrama and *zarzuela* to vaudeville. The professional stage did not only prosper from the standard works from the stages of Mexico and Madrid, but dramatic and comedic material relating directly to the culture of Mexicans in the Southwest was developed. In fact, the greatest box-office successes were those involving the production of plays and *revistas* that reflected Mexican history and society in California and the Southwest.[10] In Los Angeles, a healthy cadre of playwrights developed to supply the stages with original scripts and librettos that dealt with the epic of California history, such as Adalberto Elías González' *Ramona* and *La Conquista de California*; discrimination and the clash of cultures, as in Brígido Caro's *Joaquín Murieta* and Eduardo Carrillo's *El proceso y muerte de Aurelio Pompa*, and of course, the great Repatriation, as in Antonio Helús's *Los mexicanos se van*. Caro's *Joaquín Murieta* was taken from the professional stage and produced by amateurs as a fundraiser for the Alianza Hispano Americana.[11] And Carrillo's politically sensitive play about the condemned Pompa was produced so many times that one critic finally appealed to the producers to let poor Pompa rest in peace.[12] The Pompa play was also used quite extensively to raise funds for the accused's defense (then entitled *El proceso de Aurelio Pompa*), as well as to raise funds for his widow after his execution.[13] Another work by Brígido Caro, *México y los Estados Unidos*, was a dramatic response to Calvin Coolidge's insulting statements about Mexico in 1927. A play about about Repatriation, Gabriel Navarro's *Los emigrados*, written in 1930, was promoted as a drama "fundado en una base del absoluto realismo."[14] Antonio's Helú's *Los mexicanos se van*, tauted realismo."[14] Antonio's Helú's *Los mexicanos se van*, tauted by the June 13 and 20, 1932, editions of *La Opinión*, as an important play by a local author, openly criticizes the repatriation of Mexicans from California "en que algunos de ellos eran obligados a abandonar este país." The Mexican side of the Repatriation was depicted in Juan Bustillos Oro's 1933 drama, *Los que vuelven*, whose theme was described by the February 27, 1927, edition of *La Opinión* as "el doloroso tema de la Repatriación. En sus cuadros desfilan los desventajados, los que habiéndose adaptado a un medio de comodidades en el suelo extranjero, se ven ahora viviendo una vida precaria en su propia patria, luchando por readaptarse al nuevo medio."

So popular were these plays based on California Hispanic history and the real life drama that the communities were experiencing, that in 1930 theatre impresarios banded together to try to change the royalty arrangements accorded the playwrights, as the latter were perceived by the impresarios as getting too much of the profits from the full houses that they brought in.

Whereas the full-length plays concentrated on the serious and epic dimensions of Hispanic life in California, the world of the *revista* and musical comedy treated the same topic with satire and low humor and provided an escape valve for working-class frustration. Such comics and *peladitos* as Don Chema, Guz Aguila and Roberto Soto el Panzón had been associated with the *revista* in Mexico as a forum for piquant political commentary. In fact, before emigrating to the Los Angeles stage, Roberto Soto had been persecuted and censored repeatedly in Mexico for his biting commentary on the corrupt labor leader Morones.[15]

With such talented and well known comedians as Soto, Guz Aguila and the beloved Romualdo Tirado, Los Angeles' playwrights created such librettos about immigration and culture shock as Gabriel Navarro's *Los Angeles en pijama*, Romualdo Tirado's *La pocha y el charro* and Ernesto González Jimenez' *De México a Los Angeles o Aventuras de un sastre*. The latter is a typical tale of comedy and pathos in which a humble tailor emigrates to the big city in search of fortune, but the foreign customs and that impossible language, English, only bring him to confrontations with the police. Of course, included among the broad array of *revista* topics was the Repatriation. Ironically, the topic which was potentially controversial and sad for the community, was made light of in Don Catarino's *Los repatriados*: "En esta comedia podrá usted saborear las graciosas tribulaciones de los repatriados."[16]

It was on the vaudeville stage where that underdog, the forerunner of Cantinflas, appeared: the *pelado*. And there was no more fertile material for his biting satire, his picaresque adventures and his verbal gymnastics than the conflict of Mexican and Anglo-American culture, and the appearance of his Americanized or "agringado" compatriates. Such was the song composed by Romualdo Tirado and incorporated into his *pelado* routines in Los Angeles in 1927:

> Andas por hay luciendo
> Gran automóvil
> Me llamas desgraciado
> Y muerto de hambre
> Y es que no te acuerdas
> cuando en mi rancho

Andabas casi en cueros
Y sin huaraches.
Así pasa a muchos
Cuando aprenden un poco
de americano
Y se visten catrines
Y van al baile
Y el que niega a su raza
Ni madre tiene,
Pues no hay nada en el mundo
Tan asqueroso
Como la ruin figura del renegado.
Y aunque lejos de ti,
Patria querida,
Me han echado
Continuas revoluciones,
No reniega jamás
Un buen mexicano
de la patria querida
de sus amores.[17]

But the *pelado*, who began to use *caló* and Spanglish humoristically and later evolved into the stage *pachuco*, while dearly beloved by the working class of the *colonias*, was censured by the bourgeoisie, ever mindful of impressing upon Anglos the high quality of Mexican and Hispanic culture. One offended San Antonio critic wrote of the comic hobo, ". . . 'peladito' descamisado y calamburero, que de nuevo torna a presentarse en el escenario del Nacional como avanzada de la tan decantada 'producción artística nacional' que no se entiende si no viene el 'mecapelero,' el 'corredor de loterías,' el tenorio del barrio de largos bigotes y mechón rebelde que hace de su léxico una letanía de unsuleseces y de su presentación un descrédito para el que no conozca a México."[18]

In the delicate balance of protecting the culture and language of the Mexican immigrants while maintaining wholesome entertainment for the families, especially middle class families, the theatre house itself joined the mutualist society and the church as a refuge, a community center, a place for social and political organization.

The theatres served as one of the primary institutions for raising funds for all types of community projects, for flood victims, the construction of schools and hospitals, for defense committees for Mexicans confronting the American judicial system, and for labor organizing. Besides providing the community with a good dose of psychosocial therapy through the unbridled satires at the hands of the *peladitos*, the theatres also provided some real instances of activism. Although theatre owners, impresarios and playwrights may have been elites in the community, they often identified with the plights of their working class brethren, many of whom supported the shows quite handsomely.

In 1933, at the height of the Depression, the professional theatres in Los Ángeles dedicated a percentage of their box office to support striking Mexican farmworkers.[19] The plays that were presented often dramatized the plight of the workers, such as did *La pizca de la uva*, produced at Los Angeles' Teatro Hidalgo.[20] An El Paso benefit performance for the Unión Internacional Obrera in 1935 was typical of the events for union fundraising, with the production of the very appropriate play, *El sacrificio del jornalero*, followed by organizing speeches, 21 songs and dances.

With the demise of the professional stage brought on by the Depression and the Repatriation, many of the artists that did not return to Mexico continued to exercise their profession on behalf of the community. Daniel Ferreiro Rea in Los Angeles and Manuel Cotera and Bernardo Fougá in San Antonio performed with their companies, now made up of amateurs as well as professionals, in the Catholic churches in their communities and contributed the proceeds from their performances to the church and other worthy causes. For the most part they continued to stage the most popular plays from their secular repertoire. They, along with the churches supporting and supported by the Mexican community, continued to be a refuge for their language and their culture while offering wholesome entertainment in the face of the evergrowing threat of cultural obliteration.

Could this be what Brokaw has referred to as the theatre falling exclusively into the hands of the Church and its yearly performance of the *pastorelas*?

In conclusion, from the above we have seen that the stage indeed had a multifaceted role to play in Mexican and U.S. society and politics, as well as a meeting place, a place for political and social organizing. More importantly, the stage reflected a society coming to terms with an alien environment while bemoaning the loss of a Mexico that would never be the same. The stage offered reflection, communal therapy through the opportunity for the audiences to laugh at themselves; it was a protected sanctum in which to voice frustration freely. If politics was not addressed as openly as in today's Chicano theatre, we must remember that the audiences were for the most part made up of aliens who were liable to deportation. What is noteworthy, however, is that despite the precariousness of their status, they did allow for controversy and sociopolitical commentary.

[1]In "The Origins and Development of Hispanic Theater in the Southwest," included in this collection.

[2]John W. Brokaw, "Teatro Chicano: Some Reflections," *Educational Theatre Journal*, 29/4 (December, 1977), 535.

[3]See the intensely patriotic letter from Gerardo López del Castillo, Presidente de la Junta Central de las Sociedades Mexicanas, to C. José Marcos Mugarrieta, the Mexican Consul, dated February 23, 1863, and published on the front page of the March 10, 1863, issue of *El Eco del Pacífico*. Also see "Oración Cívica Pronunciada por el C. Gerardo López del Castillo en el Puerto de San Francisco el día 16 de septiembre de 1862" in the September 18 and 20, 1862, issues of *La Voz de Méjico*. For further information on the patriotic motivation of López del Castillo in his theatrical work, see Armando María y Campos, *La dramática mexicana durante el gobierno del Presidente Lerdo de Tejada* (México: Ediciones Populares, 1946), p. 22; and Manuel Mañón, *Historia del Teatro Principal* (México: Ed. Cultura, 1932), pp. 241-243.

[4]*La Voz de Méjico*, April 3, 1862.

[5]See *The Californian*'s October 6, 1847 review of a Spanish play presented at Abrego's inn.

[6]See the José Abrego (1813-1878) archive, C-D 86 V.2, at the Bancroft Library, University of California-Berkeley.

[7]*La Opinión*, September 2, 1932.

[8]*La Opinión*, September 11, 1930.

[9]*La Opinión*, July 14, 1931.

[10]According to playwright and theatre critic, Gabriel Navarro, ". . . las mejores entradas de 1929, en el Teatro México se registraron con motivo de los estrenos de autores mexicanos radicados en Los Angeles," *La Opinión*, April 12, 1930.

[11]*La Opinión*, April 11, 1932, The Alianza Hispano Americana's amateur theatrical company also produced Caro's intensely nationalistic *La gloria de la Raza*, under the direction of the author; see *El Heraldo de México*, January 30, 1928.

[12]On March 17, 1924, the play was debuted at Los Angeles' Teatro Hidalgo, according to *La Opinión*, on March 14, 1924. This is not the only case of benefit performances to raise funds for the defense of incarcerated Mexicans. The Circo Escalante on March 29, 1927, for example raised funds for the accused Alfredo Grijalva in Phoenix, Arizona. See the "Folkloric materials" file of the Manuel Gamio Papers at the Bancroft Library of the University of California-Berkeley.

[13]See *El Heraldo de México*, May 23, 1924.

[14]*La Opinión*, December 12, 1930.

[15]John B. Nomland, *Teatro mexicano contemporáneo* (1900-1950) (México: Instituto Nacional de Bellas Artes, 1967), p. 174. Nomland's chapter, "La revista política y humorística," pp. 145-169, is an interesting discussion of the importance of politics to the Mexican *revista*. Another great Mexican comic, active in *revista* as a political satirist, was Leopoldo Beristáin, who also spent a few years on the Los Angeles stage; see Armando María Campos, *Archivo de teatro y Crónicas* (México, 1947), pp. 59-61. Even the great actresses, Virginia Fábregas and María Teresa Montoya, who also were active performers in Los Angeles and the Southwest, were involved in political theatre in Mexico; see *La influencia de la política en el teatro mexicano*," in Armando María y Campos, *Presencias del teatro. Crónicas* 1934-1936 (México: Ediciones Botas, 1937), pp. 189-194. Pablo Prida Santacilla, the author of some of the most famous *revista* librettos, in his autobiography, . . . *y se levanta el telón* (México: Ediciones Botas, 1946), pp. 60-61, states that he came to New York as an exile from Mexico because of his burlesques of political figures.

[16]*La Opinión*, July 23, 1934.

[17]"Observations, Notes and an Itinerary of Diary of a Trip to Mexico" file in Manuel Gamio Notes, ZR-5, Bancroft Library, University of California-Berkeley.

[18]*La Prensa*, September 4, 1922.

[19]*La Opinión*, June 21, 1933. The Spanish-language newspapers of the Southwest mention many titles suggestive of the labor movement and politics, such as *El túnel o Huelga de obreros*, but we have not been able to locate scripts, authors or the social and political circumstances that they relate.

[20]*La Opinión*, August 27, 1933. It was specifically noted here that the Friday, Saturday and Sunday performances would appeal especially to "las clases populares . . . que concurren al Teatro Hidalgo."

[21]*El Continental*, March 24, 1935.